FORGOTTEN NO MORE

Incredible Tales of Valor in the Korean War

SCOTT BARON

Edited by C. Douglas Sterner

Foreword by Maj. Gen. Richard Comer USAF Ret.

FOREWORD

The service and sacrifice of those who fought in Korea are less remembered than those from many of the other conflicts fought by members of the US Armed Forces. The Korean Conflict is seldom referred to as the Korean War. In fact, our service members in Korea fought in some of the fiercest combat of the 20th Century. This book provides you some up close and personal detail of some of the individuals involved.

The in-depth research into the people's lives included here will give you a real sense of the person involved in a single combat engagement. Each self-contained short story strives to provide you each participant's perspective as they were tasked with a mission, as they planned to accomplish it, and then as they performed it.

You will get to know the person's background, showing how he or she got into this position at this time, and what is it that makes this person capable and essential to their mission.

You get the sense of it. Picture being the person given a dangerous and important mission, planning it, getting ready to do it. Each story has its own suspense, taken to conclusion, and, as I said, each story is short and self-contained. You'll know very quickly how it turned out.

Along the way, you'll also learn about many of the heroes of our nation. Each worthy of admiration and story sharing with friends. The importance of remembering these folks and what they did for us cannot not be overvalued.

Keep this book on your bed's side table or on your electronic reader. When you want to read a good, true, and short story, this book has many.

Richard Comer, Major General, USAF (Retired)

June 2020

INTRODUCTION

While this book is about the Korean War, it is not a history of the Korean War. A more than sufficient number of books already exist to serve that purpose. As with most my books, it is more about people, and the amazing things they accomplish, with the events only a historical background in which their acts can be understood. That said, a basic understanding of the Korean War is sure to be useful in placing their achievements into context.

The Korean war began on June 25, 1950, when some 75,000 soldiers from the North Korean People's Army poured across the 38th parallel, the boundary between the Soviet-backed Democratic People's Republic of Korea to the north and the pro-Western Republic of Korea to the south, in an attempt to "reunify" the country.

After 158 meetings spread over two years and 17 days of negotiations, in the longest negotiated armistice in history, U.S. Army Lt. Gen. William K. Harrison, Jr., senior delegate for the United Nations Command Delegation and North Korean Gen. Nam Il, senior delegate of the Korean People's Army Delegation and the Chinese People's Volunteers, signed the Korean Armistice Agreement on July 27, 1953, which was not a peace treaty but rather a cessation of hostility. Significantly, no South Korean representative is a signatory to the agreement.

The agreement allowed the POWs to stay where they liked, drew a new boundary near the 38th parallel that gave South Korea an extra 1,500 square miles of territory and created a 2-mile-wide "demilitarized zone" (DMV) that still exists today.

The invasion of South Korea by North Korea was the first military action of what would become known as the Cold War, the ideological struggle between Communism and Capitalism.

THE WAR BY THE NUMBERS (Sources differ)

The United States spent around $67 billion on the war that lasted 3 years and 1 month.

According to the U.S. Department of Defense, 33,739 Americans deaths were "hostile" with another 2,835 deaths classified as Non-Hostile for a total of 36,574 "In-Theatre" deaths. Another 103,284 were Wounded in Action. As of February 2019, 7,667 American soldiers are still unaccounted for (Missing in Action) from the Korean War.

South Korea suffered 217,000 military killed and over 1,000,000 civilians killed. North Korea suffered 406,000 military killed with another 303,000 wounded and over 600,000 civilians killed.

Chinese "volunteers" suffered between 400,000 to 600,000 combat deaths, with another estimated 486,000 wounded while the Soviet Union sent military aid, but no troops with the exception of a small number of advisors/observers.

According to the Korean War Legacy Project, 7,245 American soldiers and airmen were captured by the Chinese and North Koreans during the Korean War. Of these American POWs, approximately 4,418 returned home 2,806 died in captivity (almost 39% of all U.S. POWs) and 21 Americans refused repatriation.

This number does not include Americans and other UN troops who were summarily murdered upon capture, estimated at 6,113 Americans according to the Potter Report.

There were 6.8 million American men and women who served during the Korean War period, June 27, 1950 to January 31, 1955 with 751 ,820 of the total, draftees. The United States sent about 90% of the troops that were sent to aid South Korea. 16 countries sent troops and 41 sent equipment or aid. Combat troops included;

United States – 302,483
Australia – 17,000
United Kingdom – 14,198
Thailand – 6,326

Canada – 6,146
Turkey – 5,453
Philippines – 1,468
New Zealand – 1,385
Ethiopia – 1,271
Greece – 1,263
France – 1,119
Colombia – 1,068
Belgium – 900
South Africa – 826
Netherlands – 819
Luxembourg – 44

During the Korean era over 120, 000 American women were on active duty. Of those, an estimated 86,300 were Korean War veterans.

In 1950 there were only 626 WAC personnel in the Far East. By 1951 there were 2,604, by 1952 there were 1,791 and in 1953 there were 1,764. Eighteen women--16 nurses and two Air Force personnel--lost their lives in the Korean War.

TABLE OF CONTENTS

A *"Body of Steel"*

CHAPTER ONE

WILLIAM F. DEAN
Highest Ranking P.O.W. in the Korean War

At dawn on June 25, 1950, North Korean troops surged across the 38th parallel in a surprise and unprovoked invasion of South Korea quickly overwhelming the weak and poorly-trained South Korean forces as it drove south toward Seoul, the capitol of South Korea.

On June 30, recognizing the extent of the threat, President Harry S. Truman ordered General of the Army Douglas MacArthur, Supreme Commander of all Allied Forces in occupied Japan, to send ground forces into Korea to support the South Koreans.

MacArthur sought Truman's approval to send in a U.S. regimental combat team (RCT) to reinforce the Koreans with a gradual build up of two divisions from Japan for a counter-offensive against the North.

Once approved, MacArthur commanded Lt. General Walton H. Walker, commanding general of the Eighth Army to order the 24th Infantry Division, on occupation duty in Japan, to Korea "with all possible speed" and Walker conveyed the order to Maj. General William F. Dean, the 24th Division's commanding officer.

The selection of Dean to lead the advance into Korea was a logical choice as he was familiar with Korea, had experience leading men in combat and had a proven record for personal courage under fire. His habit of leading from the front would result in his becoming the highest-ranking prisoner of war (POW) during the conflict in Korea.

Forgotten No More

William Frishe Dean was born in Carlyle, Illinois on August 1, 1899, one of three children of Charles Watts Dean, a dentist, and Elizabeth Frishe. He and his brother David and sister Elizabeth grew up in a comfortable middle-class home. Dean was a good student who loved reading and playing sports in the outdoors.

Dean grew up wanting to be a soldier and, in his biography, *General Dean's* Story (1954) he credits his military ambitions on a performance of the West Point Cadet Drill Team at the 1904 St. Louis Exposition, when he was 5 years old. After graduating from Carlyle High School as valedictorian, Dean applied for admission to West Point, the U.S. Military Academy, but he was not accepted.

Dean tried to enlist in the US Army, during World War 1, but because of his age he needed his parents' permission to do so and his mother refused, so Dean instead enrolled in the pre-law program at the University of California-Berkeley and joined the Reserve Officer Training Corps (ROTC).

To support himself, Dean worked as a stevedore at the San Francisco docks, a motorman aboard trolley cars and a patrolman with the Berkeley Police Department. He graduated with a Bachelor of Arts degree in June 1922, foregoing pursuing a law degree in favor of a military career.

Dean was commissioned a second lieutenant in the California Army National Guard on March 24, 1921 before being commissioned into the Regular Army on October 18, 1923. He was assigned to the 38th Infantry Regiment, 3rd Infantry Division at Ft. Douglas, Utah. A riding accident at Ft. Douglas, in which a Miss Dorothy Welch was thrown from a horse suffering a skull fracture, resulted in his introduction to her friend, Mildred Dern, who he married in 1926

2

William F. Dean

After a posting to the 42nd, then 33rd Infantry Regiments in the Canal Zone, Panama (1926-1928), and promotion to first lieutenant on November 8, 1928, Dean returned to Ft. Douglas in 1929 and attended the Infantry School at Fort Benning, Georgia, graduating in 1931.

In 1932, Dean was sent to the 30th Infantry Regiment, 3rd Infantry Division at Presidio of San Francisco, where he served as the commanding officer of the Civilian Conservation Corps (CCC) at Camp Hackamore in Northern California and later at CCC Headquarters at Redding, Ca.

Dean was promoted to captain on August 1, 1935 and attended the Command and General Staff School at Ft. Leavenworth, Kansas (1935 -36), followed by a two-year tour of duty (1936-38) assigned to the 19th Infantry Regiment, known as the "Rock of Chickamauga" Regiment, at Schofield Barracks, Oahu, Hawaii.

Upon returning to the mainland in 1938, Dean was sent to the US Army Industrial College, graduating in 1939, followed by the US Army War College at Carlisle Barracks, Pennsylvania in 1940, with a promotion to major on July 3, 1940.

Dean was working as secretary to the Army General Staff when Pearl Harbor was attacked on December 7, 1941 and Dean was promoted to the temporary rank of lieutenant-colonel on December 24, 1941 and colonel on August 21, 1942. On December 10, 1942, he was promoted to temporary brigadier general. Impatient with staff positions during a war, Dean lobbied for a command with the troops.

Dean's request was granted when in February 1944, he joined the 44th Infantry Division at Camp Claiborne, Louisiana as the Assistant Division Commander.

The division participated in the multi-divisional maneuvers in Louisiana (February 7 – April 3, 1944) before being sent to Camp Phillips, Kansas in preparation for being sent overseas.

A training accident almost resulted in Dean missing his second war. As he recalled;

Forgotten No More

"During a demonstration of flamethrowers to division officers, a flame-thrower leaked on the lieutenant operating it. In agony as the napalm set his clothing afire, he struggled to rid himself of the weapon but instead lipped the hose, spraying napalm. Another officer and I, both rushing toward him, caught the slash of fire; but I was the lucky one. Both the other men died.

I didn't even know my leg had been burned until I started to walk off after the others had been taken away in an ambulance. Then someone noticed that my trouser leg was in tatters below the knee. I too went to the hospital, but doctors saved my leg. I was still on crutches when the division sailed, but I sailed with it."

The division departed the Boston Port of Embarkation on September 5 and landing at Cherbourg, France 10 days later. Following a month of training, the 44th entered combat on October 19, relieving the 79th Infantry Division in the vicinity of Forret de Parroy, prior to the 7th Army's drive to push into the Vosges Mountains.

It was on December 8, 1944, in the vicinity of Strasbourg, France that Gen. Dean's reputation for leading from the front was first earned. As his Distinguished Service Cross citation would describe the action;

"General Dean, finding the infantry immobilized by a withering artillery barrage, and tanks and tank destroyers halted because of the demolition of an overpass leading into the town, took immediate and decisive measures. Leading the tank and tank destroyer commanders on a foot reconnaissance to determine the most favorable plan of approach, he discovered an alternate route into the town. General Dean then personally directed the movements of the armor, while on foot and exposed to the devastating fire. After deploying these weapons and directing their fire on the principal enemy positions, he personally led an infantry platoon through one concentration of artillery fire after another and succeeded in destroying the opposing enemy batteries."

When the division commander, Major General Robert Spragins was injured and sent home, Dean took over command of the division on December 29, 1944. Dean was awarded the Distinguished Service Cross (DSC), the nation's second highest award for valor, on February 9, 1945, which was followed by a promotion to major general on March 19, 1945.

The 44th continued battling its way through France, Germany and Austria, taking part in four campaigns; Northern Europe, Rhineland, Ardennes-Alsace, and Central Europe.

Following its pursuit of the retreating German Army into Austria, and the surrender of the 19th German Army at Innsbruck on May 5, 1945, the 44th was involved in processing 30,000 German POWs at the close of the war in Europe on May 8, 1945.

In 180 days of combat, the division earned 1 Medal of Honor, 36 Distinguished Service Crosses and 464 Silver Stars. Besides the DSC, Dean was awarded the Legion of Merit and the Distinguished Service Medal for his leadership of the division during the war.

After a brief period of occupation duty, the 44th returned to the United States in July 1945 in preparation for deployment to the Pacific Theater and participation in Operation Coronet, with the 44th invading Honshu, Japan. The dropping of the atomic bombs on the Japanese cities of Hiroshima on August 6 and Nagasaki on August 9 made the invasion of Japan unnecessary, saving millions of Japanese and American lives. The Japanese surrendered on September 2, 1945, bringing WW II to an end.

Following the end of the war, Dean oversaw the division's drawdown until he was relieved of command and he returned to Ft. Leavenworth assigned to the faculty at the Command and General Staff School.

In October 1947, Dean was sent to Seoul, South Korea and appointed commander of all military forces in Korea, and deputy to Lieutenant General John R. Hodge, then commander of the US Army Military Government in Korea. Dean was responsible for overseeing the first election in Korea's 4,000-year history and assuring that the South Korean civil government functioned before it was turned over to the Koreans and military occupation ended.

Dean would later recall "I had over-all command of such activities as police work, rice collection to make sure that the hungry population had enough to eat, operation of railroads and telegraphs. The Korean constabulary was also under my command."

Dean remained in command until August 15, 1948 when a South Korean government was elected, and the occupation ended. Placed in command of the 7th Infantry Division in Seoul overseeing its withdrawal from Korea to bases in Japan as part of the occupation forces.

In May 1949, Dean was sent to Yokohama to serve as chief of staff of the Eighth Army, under the command of Gen. Walton Walker. In October 1949, Dean took command of the 24th Infantry Division in Kokura, Kyushu, Japan. Dean recalled later his memories of June 25, 1950;

"I went to the division headquarters building after attending church, the only thing on my mind was the possibility of mail from my daughter June, then enroute to Puerto Rico with her husband, Captain Robert

Williams, or from my son Bill, who was taking examinations for… West Point. But as I headed toward the post office a duty officer hailed me. North Koreans, he said, had just crossed the 38th parallel."

With the outbreak of hostilities in Korea, Walker ordered Dean to send an advance battalion from the 24th by air to South Korea with the mission of advancing and resisting the lead elements of the North Korean People's Army (NKPA) in an effort to delay them as much as possible while the remainder of the division followed by sea to land at Pusan.

Due to the lack of a sufficient number of C-54 cargo planes in-country to transport a full regimental combat team, the delaying force was comprised of men of the 1st Battalion, 21st Regiment, a single, understrength infantry battalion numbering about 405 men.

Chosen to lead the force was Lt. Col. Charles B. Smith, an experienced combat commander and 1939 West Point graduate. Present on Oahu when the Japanese attacked Pearl Harbor, Smith would now command the first American troops to engage the enemy in Korea.

William F. Dean

Lt. Gen. Walton Walker (l) and Maj. Gen. William Dean confer in Korea

Named "Task Force Smith", it was certain to face a numerically superior force, and it would do so understrength, with no tank support, no forward air controllers, no engineers or medical support, no air defense assets and no reconnaissance platoons, all standard elements of a RCT.

Dean's orders to Smith read *"When you get to Pusan, head for Taejon. We want to stop the North Koreans as far from Pusan as we can. Block the main road as far north as possible. Make contact with General Church. If you can't find him, go to Taejon and beyond if you can. Sorry I can't give you more information—that's all I've got. Good luck, and God bless you and your men!"*

On July 1, Task Force Smith landed in Pusan and advanced north with the mission of delaying the NKPA advance while additional U.S. troops arrived in the country to form a stronger defensive line to the south.

After several delays caused by a variety of circumstances, Dean landed in Taejon, Korea on July 3. Taejon was well south of the battle line and an obvious choice for a defensive headquarters. He and the Assistant Division Commander, Brigadier General John H.

Forgotten No More

Church, struggled with the task of moving the 24th Division piecemeal to Korea.

Smith set up his command at Pyeongtaek, about 15 miles south of Osan and on July 4, his command was reinforced by elements of the 52nd Field Artillery consisting of 134 men and six 105-mm. howitzers under the command of Lt. Col. Miller Perry. Just after midnight on July 5, Task Force Smith moved out heading north to Osan in a heavy rain and they were delayed by muddy roads clogged by fleeing civilians and ROK troops and arrived at 3am. They began to dig in, setting up a defensive line.

Task Force Smith took up position a mile long just north of Osan on a ridgeline 300 feet above the plain to the north. The rain showed no sign of lifting, eliminating the possibility of air support.

At 7:30 a.m. the leading elements of the NKPA 107th Tank Regiment, eight Soviet T34/85 tanks, appeared down the road initiating what would become known as the Battle of Osan.

At 8:16 a.m., at a range of 4,000 yards, the American artillery fired on the forces of North Korea for the first time, but with no effect. The standard 105-mm. rounds bounced off the tanks. Perry's battery had only six high-explosive antitank (HEAT) rounds.

The 75-mm. recoilless rifles opened fire, yet despite several direct hits, they had no better luck. Nor did the 2.36-inch bazookas, firing repeatedly at practically pointblank range. The tanks attacked with impunity and their 85 mm guns and 7.62 machine guns opened fire as the tanks rolled through, moving south.

Twenty-five more T-34s followed the initial eight-tank enemy column in intervals. Perhaps fearing that Smith's men were only the forward position of a much larger force, the tanks did not stop to engage the infantry but simply fired on them in passing, leaving behind 20 Americans dead or wounded, including Perry.

After an hour Smith observed elements of the 16th and 18th Regiments of the NKPA's 4th Division, some 5,000 men in all approaching in a six-mile column of trucks and infantry, led by three tanks. When the convoy closed to within 1,000 yards, Smith and his men opened fire.

Smith's infantry inflicted heavy casualties on the advancing enemy but were eventually flanked and subjected to heavy fire. Nearly surrounded and almost out of ammunition, Smith ordered a withdrawal at 2:30 p.m.

It was during the withdrawal the Americans suffered their greatest casualties as men carrying the wounded out were cut down by enemy mortar and machine-gun fire. Some of the men broke and ran, leaving their heavy weapons and at least two dozen wounded behind. As the advancing North Koreans came upon the injured Americans, they executed them.

When the advance columns of T-34s had passed through, they had destroyed the infantry's vehicles, so Smith's surviving infantrymen had to flee on foot and the withdrawal quickly turned into a rout. Although they had inflicted 127 casualties, the task force suffered 181 casualties and was so scattered it would be largely ineffective for some time.

With Smith's force in retreat, Dean ordered the 34th Infantry Regiment, along with elements of the arriving division to delay the advance south of Osan, but the 34th was crushed at the Battle of Pyeongtaek, where only brief resistance was offered before a panicked withdrawal.

As fighting continued, it became apparent that the 24th was heavily outnumbered and that they lacked the ordnance necessary to stop the advancing T-34s. The North Koreans continued to advance as the Americans withdrew, with defeats at the Battle of Chonan on July 8 and again at the Battle of Chochiwon from July 10-12, delaying but not halting the advance.

On July 12, Dean ordered the division's three regiments, the 19th, 21st and 34th Infantry Regiments, to cross the Kum River and destroy all the bridges behind them, and to establish defensive positions around Taejon.

Dean deployed the 34th Infantry and 19th Infantry regiments in a line facing east and held the heavily battered 21st Infantry in reserve to the southeast. The division would attempt to make a stand at Taejon, the last delaying action.

Forgotten No More

From July 13-16, the greatly outnumbered 19th and 34th Regiments engaged the NKPA 3rd Division and 4th Divisions at the Kum River, just west of Taejon, suffering 650 casualties out of the 3,401 men committed there.

Dean ordered the divisional command post east to Yongdong, but Dean remained behind in Taejon, operating out of the 34th Regimental command post. On July 18, Walker ordered Dean to hold onto Taejon until July 20 so that the US 1st Cavalry Division and US 25th Infantry Division could establish defensive lines along the Naktong River, forming the Pusan Perimeter.

On July 19, North Korean forces entered Taejon, the site of the 24th Infantry Division's headquarters, and fighting was block to block as the Americans were grudgingly forced back.

Dean, lacking communication with the various elements of the division and once again displaying an inclination for leading from the front, personally led the division in its defense of Taejon in actions that would result in the award of the Medal of Honor.

In actions later cited in his Medal of Honor citation, Dean *"personally and alone attacked an enemy tank while armed only with a hand grenade. He also directed the fire of his tanks from an exposed position with neither cover nor concealment while under observed artillery and small-arms fire. When the town of Taejon was finally overrun he refused to insure his own safety by leaving with the leading elements but remained behind organizing his retreating forces, directing stragglers, and was last seen assisting the wounded to a place of safety."*

Dean and his men had numerous engagements with enemy tanks and he joined the men on the front lines, successfully hunting the T-34 tanks with the help of the new armor-piercing 3.5 inch "Super Bazookas. But there were too many tanks.

On July 20, Dean was forced to order the 34th headquarters to withdraw while he remained behind to assist with the evacuation of the remaining troops until the last 50 vehicle convoy was ready to depart the city.

Fighting its way through a North Korean roadblock, many of the vehicles were disabled by mortar and machinegun fire, forcing the

Americans to retreat on foot and Dean's small party of jeeps was separated from the main force. Many witnesses stated their last sight of Dean was him engaging a tank with his pistol.

Dean recalled in his memoirs; *"Some people who escaped from Taejon that day reported that they last had seen me firing a pistol at a tank. Well, they did, but I'm not proud of it. As that last tank passed I banged away at it with a .45; but even then, I wasn't silly enough to think I could do anything with a pistol. It was plain rage and frustration"*

Dean's party made it out of the city, but another roadblock forced them to proceed on foot, many of them wounded, slowing their progress and causing them to fall further and further behind.

"During one of the stops to rest, I thought I heard water running just off the ridge to one side. I was sure I heard it. I headed off in that direction and the next thing I knew, I was tumbling down a slope so steep that I could not stop and plunged forward and fell unconscious."

Coming to, Dean found he had a gashed head, a broken shoulder, and many bruises. For the next 36 days, Dean wandered alone in the mountains trying to reach safety, going without food and medical treatment. Dean who had weighed 210 pounds at the start of the war was reduced to 130 pounds as he wandered for the next month.

On August 25, two South Koreans pretended to guide him towards his own lines led him into a prearranged trap by North Korean soldiers at Chinan, 35 miles south of Taejon. Dean attempted to fight the North Koreans to force them kill him, but, weak from sickness and lack of food, they easily took him prisoner.

On July 22, with Dean reported Missing in Action (MIA) and believed dead, Church was promoted to major general and appointed as commander of the 24th Infantry Division. It was not until the capture of a North Korean soldier named Lee Kyu Hyun, who had served as Dean's interpreter, that it was learned that Dean might still be alive, but US high command still generally believed that Dean was dead.

With Dean still listed as MIA, Congress voted to award Dean the Medal of Honor for his actions during the defense of Taejon.

Forgotten No More

President Harry S. Truman presented the Medal of Honor to Dean's wife, son William Dean Jr. and daughter Marjorie June Dean in a White House ceremony on February 16, 1951.

An interview by an Australian journalist, Wilfred Burchett, on December 18, 1951, was the first time US authorities learned that Dean was definitively alive and was a prisoner of war.

Dean's 1,107 days of captivity included attempted escapes and resisting torture and brainwashing. He admitted considering suicide in the three years he was a prisoner, afraid that he wouldn't hold up under torture, but remained defiant during interrogations and never revealed any information.

Dean was moved several times, but admitted that, compared to other POWS, he received relatively better living conditions, but he still suffered from dysentery and poor food.

Even after the Armistice Agreement on July 27, 1953, Dean remained in North Korea as a prisoner of war for several more weeks while the armistice was worked out. He was returned to the UN forces at Panmunjom during Operation Big Switch on September 4, 1953.

Brought to Panmunjom in a Russian jeep, still wearing his blue prison uniform, Dean was greeted by cheers from the other returnees before a 45-minute ride to Freedom Village, forgoing a sedan to ride in an ambulance with four other former prisoners. He met with UN Commander General Mark Clark, other high-ranking officers and the press.

After processing, Dean was flown to Tokyo aboard a Fifth Air Force B-17 belonging to Lt. Gen. S. C. Anderson, the Fifth's commanding officer, where he would later be greeted by MacArthur.

Dean returned to the United States on October 26 as a national hero, and was given a ticker-tape parade in New York City and was presented with the Medal of Honor in Washington DC, which he wasn't aware he'd been awarded, and modestly stated *"When I think about the men who did a better job, some who died doing them, I wouldn't have awarded myself a wood star for what I did as a commander."*

William F. Dean

After serving as Grand Marshal of the Tournament of Roses Parade on January 1, 1954, Dean settled down to his new command as Deputy Commanding General of the 8th Army at the Presidio of San Francisco, a position he retained until retiring from active duty on October 31, 1955 after 32 years of service.

Dean lived quietly in San Francisco until his death on August 24, 1981 at age 82 and he is buried next to his wife in the San Francisco National Cemetery in the San Francisco Presidio.

At his retirement ceremony on the parade ground of the Presidio of San Francisco on October 31, 1950, Army Chief of Staff Gen. Maxwell D. Taylor pinned the Combat Infantryman Badge (CIB) to Dean's tunic, stating the award was presented for "ground combat against the enemy in Korea in 1950" making him only one of two generals to be awarded the CIB.

Gen. Dean with Gen. Taylor

SOURCES:

Alexander, John. Ed. *American POW Memoirs* Wipf and Stock Publishers, Eugene Or. (2007)

Davies, Lawrence E. *Gen. Dean Retires with New Honor; Becomes 2d General Officer to Receive Infantryman's Badge -- Served 32 Years*, NY Times, Nov. 1, 1955

Dean, William F. *General Dean's Story* Viking Press NYC (1954)

General Dean Returns- Stars and Stripes, September 4, 1953

Forgotten No More

Tucker, Spencer C., Pierpaoli, Paul G. Ed. *The Encyclopedia of the Korean War: A Political, Social, and Military* ABC-CLIO, Santa Barbara, Ca. (2010)

CHAPTER TWO

JACK C. ARAKAWA

Marched his "Prisoners" to Freedom

It was a warm Friday morning at 7 am on November 10, 1950, as Lea Arakawa stood holding the hand of her 4 years old son Jack and holding her 2-year-old daughter Marylou in her arms. Beside her stood her in-laws, Mr. and Mrs. Makari Arakawa.

Standing in the terminal of Honolulu Airport in Hawaii, they watched as a Pan American airliner, chartered by the Military Air Transport Service (MATS) taxied down the runaway. As he came down the steps, Corporal Jack C. Arakawa looked upon his family for the first time in over two years, but even more remarkable, he had returned from the dead.

The Arakawa family had been notified on July 24, 1950 that Pfc Arakawa had been killed in action on July 16 at Taejon, Korea and Mrs. Arakawa, an Italian war bride, had even received a letter of condolence from President Harry S. Truman. He was also awarded a posthumous Bronze Star.

Unknown to the "widow" and the United States government until three weeks earlier, Arakawa had been taken prisoner on July 17, and the circumstances of his escape would make national headlines and help document North Korean war crimes against American POWs.

Jack Chuichi Arakawa was born in Honolulu, Hawaii on November 5, 1920, one of seven children of Mr. and Mrs. Makari Arakawa. He dropped out of school and in 1942, according to his draft registration, he was employed by McCabe, Hamilton and

Forgotten No More

Renny, working as a stevedore on the docks, unloading cargo from ships.

In March of 1943, Arakawa enlisted in the U.S. Army and after basic training was assigned to the 442nd Regimental Combat Team (RCT), a unit comprised entirely of Nisei, second-generation Japanese-Americans.

Initially, Americans of Japanese descent were prohibited from serving in the military and those serving were discharged. Martial law was declared in Hawaii and consideration was given to interning them like what was being done on the west coast of the United States but with one-third the population of Japanese ancestry, internment was deemed "impractical".

Finally, an order dated January 22, 1943, allowing the enlistment of Japanese-Americans, directed, *"All cadre men must be American citizens of Japanese ancestry who have resided in the United States since birth"* and *"Officers of field grade and captains furnished under the provisions of subparagraphs a, b and c above, will be white American citizens. Other officers will be of Japanese ancestry insofar as practicable."* In accordance with those orders, the 442d Combat Team was activated February 1, 1943.

After training at Camp Shelby, Mississippi, the regiment sailed from Hampton Roads, Virginia on 1 May 1944 and landed at Anzio on May 28. The 442nd joined the 100th Battalion in Civitavecchia north of Rome on June 11, 1944, attached to the 34th Infantry Division. The newly-formed Nisei unit went into battle on June 26, 1944 at the village of Belvedere in Suvereto, Tuscany.

In his time with the 442nd Arakawa was assigned to Weapons Platoon, H Company as a machine-gunner and fought in the Rome-Arno, Southern France, Northern Apennines and Po Valley campaigns, earning the award of a Bronze Star and Purple Heart.

While stationed in Florence, Italy, he met and married his wife Lea, and brought her back to Honolulu with him upon his honorable discharge in November 1946 after 3 years, 8 months service. However, "bored" with civilian life, Arakawa reenlisted in December 1947.

Assigned to C Company, 1st Battalion, 19th Infantry Regiment, Arakawa departed for Japan in August 1948, leaving his family for occupation duty at Camp Chickamauga, Kyushu.

By all accounts, Occupation duty was pleasant living. Quartered in comfortable barracks, good American food in well-equipped dining halls, church services in attractive chapels, movie theatres with the latest films, daily news broadcasts from the States, a well-stocked post exchange, leisure-time activities at Red Cross clubs, and competitive sports.

Additionally, soldiers attended the Division School Center, at Kokura, for training as radio operators, cooks and bakers, clerk-typists, or as armorer-artificers. Higher echelon schools are open for advanced training in welding, mechanics, and numerous other fields.

Unfortunately, training for combat was minimal due to the reduction of the military budget in the post-war economy. When the North Koreans invaded the south, on June 25, 1950, the US military was caught woefully unprepared.

The 24th Infantry Division in Japan was the closest to Korea and elements of the 24th were the first US troops on the ground, arriving June 30, with the mission of delaying the North Korean advance until additional UN and American troops could arrive.

The 2nd Battalion, 19th Infantry landed at Pusan on July 2 and on July 16, Arakawa and his company were in a hastily prepared defensive position outside the South Korean town of Taejon. It would be Arakawa's first, and only, combat in Korea.

That evening, at about 8pm, as planes flew overhead, and the noise of explosions and gunfire filled the night air, Pfc Arakawa waited behind his .50 caliber machinegun watching the advance of North Korean tanks and infantry. Arakawa fired only about 500 rounds of ammunition until the gun jammed.

Forgotten No More

19ᵗʰ Infantry Regiment in the mountains near Seoul in July, 1950

As his posthumous Bronze Star citation described it, Arakawa's position was *"subjected to intense attacks from waves of enemy infantry supported by small arms, machinegun, and mortar fire. Completely disregarding fire to which he was subjected, Arakawa fired his machinegun at the enemy until it exploded, deafening and partially blinding him. After this accident, he picked up an automatic rifle and continued to fire at the enemy. His calmness, courage and perseverance enabled a number of his fellow soldiers to evacuate the position under attack as his company withdrew. He continued to fire at the enemy until he was killed."*

Arakawa later stated that he lost consciousness when a bullet grazed his chest. He blacked out, falling into a rice paddy. Left for dead by North Korean soldiers, he was left unmolested and after darkness managed to make his way to the hills. Later, he slipped into a small village held by North Korean troops and tried to evade capture by deceiving them into believing he was a farmer.

Arakawa had shaved his head before leaving Japan and had passed unnoticed in the village. *"The North Koreans all shave their heads,* "he later explained, *"while the South Koreans wear their hair long."*

After traveling for two miles, his masquerade was discovered, and he was taken prisoner. Korean officers who questioned him initially believed him to be a Japanese soldier and his ability to communicate with his captors in Japanese probably saved him from being executed, like a number of American POWs that were murdered by the North Koreans.

For 38 days, he and other American prisoners were forced to carry ammunition and supplies for their captors, sometimes marching for 16 straight hours in one day with only a few breaks. They were fed rice and hot soup twice a day. Once in a great while they got a bit of pork and beef.

During this period, Arakawa said he came into contact with five other Hawaiian soldiers and some mainland Nisei troops captured by North Koreans. In early September, Arakawa was transferred to a makeshift prison cam in Seoul where he and other POWs were subjected to daily interrogations and mandatory "classes" on the evils of capitalism. There was also pressure to defect to the NKPA, with promises of *"better food, sake, medical care, parties, better housing and a woman".*

Following the landing at Inchon on September 15, plans were made to evacuate all POWs north of the 38th parallel and on September 25, as American led forces regained control of Seoul in street-to street fights, Arakawa and 376 other POWs began what would become known as the "Korean Death March", a 270-mile forced march to Pyongyang.

As the malnourished prisoners were marched north, many of them wounded, their NKPA guards executed those who could not keep up, and they were frequently mistaken strafed by friendly aircraft mistaking them for retreating enemy troops. By the time they reached the North Korean capital, approximately 80 POWs had died from malnutrition, disease, summary execution and friendly fire.

Forgotten No More

Arriving in Pyongyang on October 10, with American-led forces in close pursuit, the prisoners were advised that they would be moved by railcars closer to the Manchurian border. That was when Arakawa and four other POWs resolved to attempt an escape, hoarding their meager rations in preparation.

On October 14, approximately 370 POWs were assembled for a march to the railway station for transport to a camp near the Yalu River. At some point, Arakawa and four others were able to dash into an alley and hide, knowing that if they were caught they would be immediately executed.

Finding a North Korean Army coat and hat, discarded by a retreating and donned it and proceeded to march his "prisoners" through the streets and roadblocks, assisted by his ethnic appearance and knowledge of Korean.

Approaching a larger checkpoint on the city outskirts, and fearing his limited Korean would give them away, Arakawa recalled *"I proceeded to march the men to the entrance of the main road block at a fast pace. Approximately ten feet from the main gate of the road block, I shouted "Air Raid" in the Korean language, at the same time we charged the gate using knives we had made as well as broken bottles."*

Fighting their way through and fleeing into the night, the five hid in an abandoned house for 6 days, their only food; 15 pounds of flour, 2 apples, several slices of bread and 20 gallons of water.

On October 20, alerted by the ringing of church bells and a commotion in the streets, they cautiously emerged to greet approaching South Korean troops.

The fate of the other POWs was not as fortunate. Of the 180 POWs who traveled north, 70 died of disease, malnutrition or exposure in the sixteen-day journey in open rail cars to Manchuria.

Late in the afternoon of October 30, outside the town of Sunchon, the prisoners were taken from the railroad cars in alternate groups of approximately 40 to nearby ravines, ostensibly to receive their first food in several days. There they were ruthlessly executed by North Korean. 68 were murdered while 21 others were wounded but survived by playing dead and burrowing under the bodies.

JACK C. ARAKAWA

Pfc. John E. Martin, formerly with the 29th Regimental Combat

Team, one of the survivors of the Sunchon tunnel massacre, later testified in a Senate investigation:

"They had us all get off the train. We were all in the

tunnel there. The highest-ranking officer, two sergeants, and another corporal had already left earlier. There was some money collected up by the prisoners, supposedly to buy food. They hadn't come back yet. They told us we were going to a small house to eat and the reason we were going in groups was because it was so small.

The first group went out and the guards were gone about 20 minutes to a half hour. When they left we heard a lot of small-arms fire, but I never thought anything about it, and I don't think too many other people did either.

They came back for my group and we started out and we went down the track about 400 yards and I had fallen back to the rear * * *. My feet were pretty bad, and I had to keep falling back. I couldn't keep up with them. We went around the corner, into this ditch. They said, "Get down; the planes. Get down; the planes. So, when we all ducked down some more of them came up on us over a little rice paddy and they just opened up.

As I came around I just sat down when they started to fire, and I fell forward on the embankment. I was right just about at one of their feet and I suppose he thought I was hit and was firing over my head at other people. Then another fellow fell just about across me, more or less on my back, and when they did come down in the ditch and check they were in a hurry. They didn't get all the way down to me before they went back up."

Arakawa and the other's decision to escape most likely saved their lives. They were taken to a field hospital near Taejon and then shipped to Fukuoka Hospital in Tokyo. The 5'4 Arakawa had lost 40 pounds in his 89 days as a POW.

On October 21, Arakawa's family received the incredible news that he was alive, and they were waiting to greet him when he arrived in Honolulu on November 10. Upon arrival and after taking accumulated leave, Arakawa was assigned as the Fort Shafter chaplain's driver.

Forgotten No More

On February 17, 1951, in a ceremony at Schofield Barracks, Hawaii, Major General P.W. Clarkson, Deputy Commanding General of Army Forces-Pacific presented Cpl. Arakawa with a Silver Star, upgrading his Bronze Star, and an additional Purple Heart.

Arakawa remained in the Army, retiring in 1964 as a staff sergeant. He was working as a cargo clerk for the US Air Force at Hickham Field when he passed away on March 26, 1973 at age 52.

He was buried March 30, 1973 at the National Memorial Cemetery of the Pacific before 150 mourners with Buddhist rites and military honors.

It is said that on occasion, Arakawa would pull out and review accounts and photos from his first funeral.

SOURCES:

Chinnery, Phillip D. *Korean Atrocity! Forgotten War Crimes 1950-1953* Naval Institute Press, Annapolis MD (2000)

Cpl. Jack Arakawa, Once Listed among Korean War Dead, Returns Honolulu Star Bulletin Friday, November 10, 1950

Gauthier, Brandon K. *The strange story of one Korean War POW* https://www.nknews.org/2014/03/the-strange-story-of-one-korean-war-pow/

Hawaiian Nisei GI Reported Killed, One Missing In Action, Pacific Citizen Salt Lake City (UT) August 5, 1950

McDaniel, William Thomas Jr. *The Major – Senior Officer in Charge Commanding Fellow Prisoners of War* Xlibrus US (2011)

Nelson, Lyle. *Death of a Korean POW Recall Strange Story*, Honolulu Star Bulletin (HI) March 31, 1973

Oahu War Hero to be Decorated at Schofield Ceremony Honolulu Star Bulletin (HI) Feb. 16, 1951

CHAPTER THREE

RUBY BRADLEY
Most Decorated US Servicewoman

Following the amphibious UN counter-offensive at Incheon in September 1950, UN forces invaded North Korea in October 1950 and moved rapidly towards the Yalu River, the border with China.

On October 19, Chinese forces of the People's Volunteer Army (PVA) crossed the Yalu and the surprise intervention by the Chinese triggered a retreat of UN forces back below the 38th Parallel.

As 100,000 Chinese soldiers surged south, the 171st Evacuation Hospital was just setting up in Pyongyang and found itself right in path of the advancing Chinese and North Korean forces.

As aircraft and ambulances scrambled to evacuate wounded and staff out of harm's way, the Chief Nurse, Major Ruby Bradley, ordered her subordinates to evacuate with the first group of evacuees but remained behind to supervise the withdrawal of the remaining wounded, remaining until the end of November.

Bradley refused to evacuate until the last of the sick and wounded had been loaded aboard the last plane. As the last wounded soldier was being loaded, and she ran up the ramp, she could her small arms fire striking the fuselage.

As the aircraft taxied down the runway, and she glanced out the side window, she watched an artillery shell explode, blowing up her ambulance. She later recalled *"You got to get out in a hurry when you have somebody behind you with a gun."*

Forgotten No More

For Bradley, it was not her first time under fire, having served during WWII and having survived 37 months as a prisoner of war.

Major Ruby Bradley

Ruby Bradley was born in Spencer, West Virginia on December 19, 1907 the fifth of six children (4 girls, two boys) born to Fred O. Bradley and Bertha Welch, and she grew up on the family farm.

In 1926, at age 19, she graduated from Biddle State College in Glenville, West Virginia with a teaching certificate, returned home to Spencer and for the next 4 years, she taught students in grades 1-8 in a one-room school house in Roane County.

Rural teaching jobs were scarce, and she was lucky to have work, especially a job that paid $50 a month, but a desire for adventure prompted her to follow her younger sister Sally, an Army nurse at Walter Reed Army Hospital, into the medical field.

Bradley applied to the Philadelphia General Hospital School of Nursing, a charity hospital which nonetheless was ranked as one of the greatest municipal hospitals in the world.

The program was highly selective, especially so during the Depression, and included an interview, references, and a physical exam, but her two years of college and a letter from her minister favorably impressed the committee. Bradley was accepted into the program on July 1, 1930 and graduated as a surgical nurse in 1933.

Rural nursing opportunities were few during the Depression, so on December 18, 1933, Bradley accepted a position as a civilian staff nurse with the Civilian Conservation Corps (CCC) working at Walter Reed Army Hospital in Washington DC.

Major Ruby Bradley

Following in her sister's footsteps, Bradley enlisted in the Army Nurse Corps (ANC) on October 16, 1934 and was sworn in as a second lieutenant and assigned to Walter Reed as an Army Nurse where she remained for the next six years.

The Army Nurse Corps dates back to 1901, but it wasn't until the Army Reorganization Act of 1920 that Army nurses were granted "relative rank" with insignia identical to commissioned officers in the Army, but the corps was not part of the regular Army. Nurses received no military basic training, were paid 2/3 of an officer's salary, and enlisted men were not required to salute them.

While nurses were not commissioned officers, their relative standing in the army corresponded to that of commissioned officers. The "assimilated ranks" of lieutenant, captain, and major were authorized. The superintendent (corps chief) was appointed a major, the assistant superintendent and directors pinned on captains' bars, chief nurses were selected as first lieutenants and staff nurses, the majority, were appointed as second lieutenants.

It was not until February 26, 1944 that Congress passed a bill granting nurses full military rank, but only for the duration of the war and six months.

On November 24, 1939, Bradley received orders for her first overseas assignment to the Philippines, a coveted two-year assignment. She and three other nurses reported to the Port of Embarkation and departed aboard the transport USS *Henderson* (AP-1) in January 1940 and arriving in the Philippines on Valentine's Day 1940.

The USS *Henderson* was converted to a hospital ship and commissioned as USS *Bountiful* (AH-9) in 1943.

After a brief orientation at the Sternberg General Hospital in Manila, Bradley was sent to the station hospital at Fort Mills on the island of Corregidor.

A year later, on February 14, 1941, Bradley was transferred to Camp John Hay in Baguio, in Luzon's Cordillera Central Mountains, a retreat for wealthy Americans 200 miles north of Manila.

Forgotten No More

On the morning of December 8, 1941, Bradley was on duty at the hospital sterilizing instruments for that mornings surgery when she was ordered to report to the headquarters. She was informed that all surgeries were canceled.

5,299 miles away, and across the international dateline, the Japanese had attacked United States military forces at Pearl Harbor, Territory of Hawaii. The country was now at war with Japan.

As she reported to the surgeon's office for further directions, planes flew overhead so low that she could see the pilots staring down at her, and the big red circles on the wings identifying them as Japanese. As bombs began to fall, she noted the time; 8:19 AM. Shortly afterward, the first casualties began arriving at the hospital.

From December 8 until December 23, Bradley and the other nurses endured almost constant air attacks while working sixteen-hour shifts in the hospital tending a growing number of sick and injured soldiers, sailors and civilians.

The main Japanese attack on Luzon began early on the morning of December 22nd as 43,110 men of the 48th Division and one regiment of the 16th Division, supported by artillery and approximately 90 tanks, landed at three points along the east coast of Lingayen Gulf.

As the Army evacuated and the Japanese took over the camp on Dec. 23, Bradley, a doctor and another nurse, Maj. Beatrice Chambers, like many other Americans who refused to surrender, headed into the mountains to evade capture.

In one day, they hiked 30 kilometers along a dirt track through difficult mountainous terrain to a lumbering camp. Their objective was Manila, however, all the main roads to Manila had been blocked. Bridges had been destroyed by the departing American forces and Japanese planes patrolled every major access to the city. They hid in the hills.

Accounts differ as to whether they were betrayed, surrendered or were captured, but in any event, Bradley and Chambers were the first US Army nurses to be taken prisoners of war by the Japanese.

Major Ruby Bradley

The first servicewomen taken prisoner were five Navy nurses (Chief Nurse Marion Olds, and Lieutenants (junior grade) Leona Jackson, Lorraine Christianson, Virginia Fogerty and Doris Yetter) captured on Guam on December 10, 1941.

At their old post, Camp John Hay, the first internment camp was established. More than 500 civilians, men, women and children, were crowded into one building.

The building which the Japanese selected was an old barrack building that had not been used by the American Army for several years because it had been declared unsafe for occupancy. Designed for 50 men, the building now housed ten times that number.

The internees consisted of missionaries, miners and the two Army nurses, Bradley and Chambers. The missionaries had been evacuated from China and had established a language school in the Philippines while awaiting the opportunity to return to China. The miners, some of whom were actually lumbermen, had been living and working near Baguio.

The barrack was so crowded that the only walking space was a small aisle down the center. Bedding was on the floor and each bed was rolled into a bundle during the day to allow for more space. After a few weeks, an additional building was obtained for male internees.

As Bradley recalled *"It may be said that camp life was more bearable for the medical personnel than for any other, as these people performed essential services consistent with their previous professional training. "*

Bradley also recalled the difficulties of treating the sick and wounded under restrictions imposed by their captors; *"Every activity of the internees had to be approved by the Japanese army commander. This was a frustrating situation and contributed to feelings of rebelliousness among the internees who were U.S. citizens. Everything was regimented by the Japanese; admission of patients to the hospital; determination of the number of doctors, nurses and attendants who could work in the hospital at any one time"*

On April 23, 1943, Bradley was transferred to the civilian internment camp at Camp Holmes in Baguio. The camp, also known as Camp #3, contained 500 civilians.

Forgotten No More

On one occasion, shortly after the Japanese relocated their prisoners to Camp Holmes, Bradley, a doctor and a dentist were driven back to Camp John Hay by a Japanese soldier to locate toilet paper.

While searching the hospital, Bradley located drugs, including World War I-era morphine, and surgical instruments (consisting of nine Kelly hemostats, six mosquito hemostats, two pairs of surgical scissors, two abdominal retractors, two knife handles, four packages of blades, two handling forceps and one uterine forceps)

At great risk should she be caught, Bradley smuggled them into the camp, then feigned the need to use the bathroom, running inside and hiding them, prior to being searched.

During 37 months of captivity, Bradley assisted in 230 major operations and the delivery of 13 babies. *"The Japanese thought it was wonderful we could do all this without any instruments."*

During her time in captivity, Bradley's weight dropped to 85 pounds, due in part to her sharing her meager rations with the camp's hungry children. Her loose uniform facilitated her smuggling activities.

On September 20, 1943, Bradley was transferred to Santo Tomas Internment Camp in Manila, where she remained until it was liberated. Conditions deteriorated as the war progressed. *"There were several deaths a day, mostly the older ones, who just couldn't take it."*

At the Santo Tomas camp, Bradley and the other imprisoned nurses who provided them with medical treatment were dubbed the "Angels in Fatigues."

In January 1944, administration of the internment camp was transferred from Japanese civil authorities to the Japanese Imperial Army, and conditions in the camp deteriorated so bad that by January 1945, the daily ration was down to 700 calories.

Major Ruby Bradley

Bradley and other nurses being repatriated

On February 3, 1945 after three years of captivity, U.S. troops stormed the gates of Santo Tomas Internment Camp and liberated Bradley and her fellow prisoners.

Bradley returned home to a hero's welcome and many honors, including the awards, like all the POW nurses, of a Bronze Star, the Asiatic-Pacific Campaign Medal with 2 Battle Stars, Presidential Unit Citation with 2 oak leaf clusters, and both the Philippine Liberation and Philippine Defense Ribbon with one battle star.

After a brief visit home, Bradley was back to work on July 4, 1945 as the Assistant Chief Nurse at Ft. Myer, Virginia where she remained until shortly before the end of the war, on August 12. Brief postings followed at McGuire General Hospital in Richmond, the station hospital at Ft. Eustis, Virginia and Letterman General Hospital in San Francisco. By February 17, 1949, Bradley was back at Walter Reed in Washington DC.

Following her repatriation, Bradley was promoted to 1st Lieutenant (AUS) on February 18, 1945 and Captain (AUS) on October 27 of the same year. On August 19, 1947, her commission was transferred to the Regular Army (RA)

Forgotten No More

On May 15, 1950, Bradley was promoted to major and on July 17 reported to Ft. Bragg, N.C. as Chief Nurse of the 171st Evacuation Hospital.

On June 25, hostilities broke out in Korea and by August 27, the 171st arrived at Camp Hakata, Kyushu, Japan where it remained, organizing, until landing at Taegu, South Korea on September 21, one of the first medical units "in-country".

The 171st moved north behind US forces, but only barely behind the lines, arriving in Pyongyang on Halloween, October 31 and Bradley remained there during the Chinese counter-offensive, and evacuated on the last plane out on November 30.

The 171st arrived in Yongdongpo on December 6, and relocated to Camp Kokura, Kyushu, Japan on December 18, 1950. Bradley was detached for temporary duty with the 361st Station Hospital in Tokyo on January 13, 1951 but returned to the 171st on June 19.

On July 12, Bradley received orders assigning her to Headquarters, Eighth Army and on August 1, 1951 she assumed the duties of Chief Nurse, Eighth Army with a promotion to lieutenant colonel on July 23, 1952, the highest-ranking nurse in Korea.

On June 20, 1953, with peace talks underway at Panmunjom, Bradley departed Korea and Gen. Maxwell Taylor, Commanding General of the 8th Army ordered an international parade and review in her honor, recognizing her three years of service in Korea, a first for a military nurse.

Bradley's post-Korea assignments included Director of Nursing, Headquarters 3rd Army at Ft. McPherson, Ga., where she, along with Inez Haynes and Ruby Bryant, was promoted to full colonel on March 4, 1958, the first women to achieve that rank. She next served as Chief Nurse, US Army Europe at Heidelberg, Germany and then Director of Nursing, Brooke Medical Center, Ft. Sam Houston, Texas where she retired on March 31, 1963 after almost 30 years of service.

Besides the awards previous mentioned, Bradley was awarded two Legion of Merit Medals, an additional Bronze Star and two Army

Commendation Medals among others, in total 34 awards. She was also presented the Florence Nightingale Medal, the International Red Cross' highest honor.

Although "retired", Bradley continued nursing in Roane County, West Virginia until 1980. On May 28, 2002, at age 94, Bradley suffered a heart attack while living in a nursing home in Hazard, Kentucky.

Bradley was laid to rest on July 2 at Arlington National Cemetery with full military honors, including six white horses drawing her caisson, followed by a riderless horse, a military band and a 21-gun salute.

In 2013, Nancy Polette wrote a book about Bradley entitled Angel in Fatigues. When asked her feelings about being America's most decorated military woman, Bradley would just shrug and modestly answer *"It was all in a day's work."*

SOURCES:

Bradley, Ruby G. *Prisoners of War in the Far East*
https://history.amedd.army.mil/ancwebsite/bradley/bradley.html

Bullough, Vern L. Ed. *American Nursing: A Biographical Dictionary: Volume 3* Springer Publishing Company, (Jan 1, 2004)

Norman, Elizabeth M. *We Band of Angels – The Untold Story of American Nurses Trapped on Bataan* Simon & Schuster (1999)

Nye, Logan. *America's 'most decorated woman' fought from the Philippines to Korea*
https://www.wearethemighty.com/articles/americas-most-decorated-woman-fought-from-the-philippines-to-korea

Polette, Nancy. *Angel in Fatigues: The Story of Colonel Ruby G. Bradley - The most decorated woman in the history of the US Army* Blessinks Pub. (April 9, 2013)

https://history.amedd.army.mil/ancwebsite/bradley/bradleyres.html

Forgotten No More

CHAPTER FOUR

H. RICHARD HORNBERGER
The Real "Hawkeye Pierce"

One reason the Korean War has become known as "The Forgotten War" is the general lack of knowledge regarding the conflict, and what knowledge there is has been shaped primarily by popular culture.

Many Americans in the 1970's, and since, shaped their perceptions of the Korean War influenced by the popular television sitcom M*A*S*H* (1972-1983) which was based on the 1970 Robert Altman film of the same name, itself based on Richard Hooker's 1968 novel **MASH**: *A Novel About Three Army Doctors.*

The story is set in Korea during the war, centering around a group of army surgeons assigned to the fictional 4077th MASH (Mobile Army Surgical Hospital) and is a black comedy about trying to remain sane under insane conditions.

The author, Richard Hooker, is a pseudonym for H. Richard Hornberger and is loosely based on his experiences as a drafted army surgeon serving with the 8055th MASH in Korea during the war. Hornberger modeled the character, Captain Benjamin Franklin "Hawkeye" Pierce on himself and other characters were composites of people he served with.

Hiester Richard Hornberger Jr. was born to Hiester and Verena Hilton Hornberger in Trenton, New Jersey on February 1, 1924. To distinguish him from his father, he began using H. Richard at an early age. The family moved from New Jersey to Bremen, Maine to be closer to his mother's family.

Forgotten No More

Hornberger attended high school at The Peddle School, a college preparatory school in Hightstown NJ, graduating in 1941, and then attending Bowdoin College in Brunswick, Maine. *"I had the lowest marks of any pre-med student in the class"* he recalled, but the recommendation of his chemistry teacher got him admitted to Cornell Medical School in Manhattan, New York City.

Voluntary enlistments of doctors and dentists had not kept up with the expansion of the military and there was an urgent need due to the Korean War and Congress passed Public Law 779 in September 1950, also known as the Doctors Draft Act of 1950.

Rather than call up large number of physicians with military experience from World War II, the Act The law set up a system of priorities in which those with the least amount of service would be called first. Former students who received part or all of their training at government expense but had served less than 90 days in World War II were called first; second called were those with more than 90 days but less than 21 months; third were those who got their training at other than government expense but who never served in the armed forces or public health service; and finally those who got their training at other than government expense and served in the armed forces.

As a result, the military lost the most experienced physicians who could have guided and trained residents and other medical personnel during the early stages of the war. To make matters worse, many of the newly recruited physicians and nurses received no training in combat medicine or military culture.

As a result, military discipline and decorum was not always a priority with the drafted medics. As Hornberger recalled in an interview, they would *"Do the job well and after that, do as we please. We were out there in the middle of nowhere. What could they do? Fire us?"*

H. Richard Hornberger

Capt. H.R. Hornberger (L) in front of "The Swamp"

Hornberger was working his internship as a surgeon when he was drafted into the US Army in 1950. He was commissioned a captain in the US Army Medical Corps and was sent to Korea in the fall of 1951, assigned to the 8055th MASH, located near the 38th parallel. The 8055th was the first medical unit to arrive in Korea, landing at Pusan, South Korea on July 6, 1950.

The 8055th MASH was a 60-bed mobile hospital with a staff consisting of 10 medical officers, 12 nursing officers, and 89 enlisted soldiers of assorted medical, like corpsmen, and non-medical specialties such as clerks and cooks. It was initially under the command of Lt. Col. George Rumer. *"There were about 30 Koreans assigned to our unit"* Dr. Harold Secor, another 8055th surgeon recalled. *"We had several jeeps, two ambulances, and three or four trucks and were generally four to five miles behind the front lines."*

The "Mobile" in MASH was the challenge given the poor roads and rugged mountainous terrain. But MASH units were

Forgotten No More

required to be ready to move within 6 hours and be fully operational after arriving at the new location.

They operated, literally, out of tents and as one surgeon later described it, "*We weren't on the front lines, but they were close. It was hot in the summer and colder than cold in the winter. The operating room consisted of stretchers balanced on carpenter's sawhorses.*"

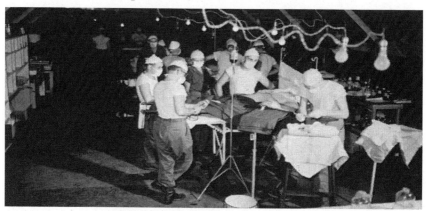

8055th MASH surgeons in action

Dr. Dale Drake, an anesthesiologist with the 8055th recalled in a USA Today interview in 2013 "*What characterized the fighting in Korea was that you would have a period of a week or 10 days when nothing much was happening, then there would be a push. When you had a push, there would suddenly be a mass of casualties that would just overwhelm us.*"

The war was slowing down by early 1952, but the war was still going on, and some of the heaviest fighting was yet to be.

The 8055th by this time was located near Uijongbu, a city that had seen heavy fighting in the first days of the war, about 10-15 miles behind the lines (depending where the line was that week).

The concept of tactical mobility for surgical units was not new in Korea. Mobile Army Surgical Hospitals resulted from the experiences in WWII when the use Litter jeeps and field ambulances resulted in rapid evacuations to division field hospitals that had been moved as close to the front as possible.

H. Richard Hornberger

This resulted in improvements in immediate aid and patient care and increased the chances for survival. The time from wounding to emergency surgery decreased dramatically. The next step was to fill the gap in the evacuation chain between the aid stations and the evacuation hospitals.

It had to be an independent unit with its own vehicles and its own chain of command. Plans for these new MASH units, with their own vehicles and chain of command, were announced in August 1945, and the first actual unit was organized in 1948. They were 60-bed, truck-borne forward units that could be set just beyond the artillery range of the enemy.

Eventually there were five MASH units in Korea and the Table of Organization called for each to be staffed by three surgeons and three non-surgeon assistants, two anesthesiologists, one radiologist, two internists, three general duty medical officers, twelve nurses, two medical service corps officers, one warrant officer, and 93 enlisted personnel. This varied widely during the war.

In the early days of the war, a MASH unit treated up to 150 patients in a day, so they were quickly reorganized into 200-bed units. Once a patient was stable, he would be transferred to one of three semi-mobile 400-bed hospitals capable of longer-term care. The next stop would be a permanent field hospital, a station hospital, or a hospital ship, followed by evacuation to a U.S. hospital.

Korea was the first conflict to use helicopters as "air ambulances" to evacuated casualties, primarily using the Bell H-13 helicopters for Medevac (Medical Evacuation), transporting two patients on the skids.

MASH surgeons pioneered advances in vascular surgery. Dr. Steven G. Friedman, writing in the August 2017 Journal of Vascular Surgery credited Hornberger as one of the first to develop these new techniques.

Hornberger pioneered a kind of surgery that was prohibited during the war. "*Hornberger possessed the courage and audacity to attempt arterial repair when it was forbidden and by one account, he may have been the first,*" Friedman wrote.

Forgotten No More

At the time, it was against U.S. Army regulations for surgeons to do anything but close off a blood vessel in the case of an injury to the vascular system, or blood vessels. But the realities of war wounds made this intolerable to Hornberger and other surgeons who found themselves banned from repairing damaged arteries.

In 1951, Hornberger's colleagues told Friedman, surgeons at the MASH unit decided to follow their Hippocratic oath to do no harm rather than Army regulations and they began repairing arteries against regulations.

Friedman wrote *"Arterial repair was first performed in MASH 8055 during the summer of 1951. The precise number and authors of the initial cases remain vague because of the surgeons' unwillingness to record them. The first repairs were experimental and were performed on Chinese and North Korean prisoners of war. A second reason for nonreporting was that surgeons feared judicial reprisal for violating military policy."*

Reports by visiting surgeons about the success of arterial repair put pressure on military medical leaders to change the policy, which they eventually did, resulting in rapid advances in suture material and clamps.

Hornberger also practiced what became known as "Meatball Surgery" which was described as performing an adequate job at high speed as opposed to refinement and meticulousness.

Writing to his father in the pilot episode of the M*A*S*H TV series, his alter-ego Hawkeye wrote *"We're not concerned with the ultimate reconstruction of the patient. We only care about getting the kid out of here alive enough for someone else to put on the fine touches. We work fast and we're not dainty, because a lot of these kids who can stand two hours on the table just can't stand one second more. We try to play par surgery on this course. Par is a live patient."*

MASH units contributed to improvements in resuscitation and trauma care, patient transport, blood storage and distribution, patient triage and evacuation. MASH units would play a significant role in reducing battlefield mortality rates from 4% in WW II to 2.5% in Korea.

H. Richard Hornberger

MASH units continued to be utilized during Vietnam and Desert Storm and the last MASH unit was deactivated on February 16, 2006, succeeded by the Combat Support Hospital (CSH)

Hornberger returned stateside after 18 months overseas and was honorably discharged from the Army. He worked briefly as a doctor for the Veterans Administration before settling in Broad Cove, Maine where Hornberger built a home for his wife, two sons and two daughters. He worked as a thoracic surgeon in a private practice as well as at Thayer Hospital in Waterville Maine, working 6-7 days a week before retiring in 1988.

In 1956, partly as a way to process his experiences in the war, Hornberger began writing a manuscript of his experiences, finishing in 1959, but the manuscript was rejected 17 times before being published by William Morris and Company after revising the work assisted by legendary sportswriter W. C. Heinz, himself a veteran of Korea.

The book, *M*A*S*H*: A Novel of Three Army Doctors,* was published in 1968 with Hornberger using the pseudonym Richard Hooker, a reference to his golf game and the world was introduced to Hawkeye, "Trapper John" Hot Lips" O' Houlihan, "Radar" O' Reilley and Henry Blake. The novel was so highly successful that it was made into the movie, *MASH* and a TV series of the same name.

The 1970 movie M*A*S*H*, directed by Robert Altman and starring Donald Sutherland, and Elliott Gould, with Sally Kellerman, Robert Duvall, and Tom Skerritt, was nominated for five Academy Awards, including Best Picture and won for Best Adapted Screenplay. The film grossed $81.6 million at the box office.

The TV series M*A*S*H*, created by Larry Gelbart and Gene Reynolds, which ran for 11 years, from 1972-1983, had the same characters as the book and movie, this time portrayed by Alan Alda, Wayne Rogers, Loretta Swit, Larry Linville, McLean Stevenson and Gary Burghoff, reprising his movie role as "Radar" O' Reilly.

"Goodbye, Farewell and Amen" the final episode, aired on February 28, 1983, and was 2½ hours long, and according to a *New York Times* article, the final episode of *M*A*S*H* had 125 million

viewers, a record audience for a television show, and was nominated for over 100 Emmy Awards, winning 14.

Hornberger wrote two sequels to MASH; M*A*S*H Goes to Maine (1972) and M*A*S*H Mania (1977), neither of which enjoyed the commercial success of the original. Additionally, a series of 12 books based on the M*A*S*H* franchise were published, credited to "Richard Hooker and William E. Butterworth", although they were written entirely by Butterworth. Butterworth, aka W.E.B. Griffith.

While the movie and TV series made a ton of money for the producers and actors, Hornberger sold the rights for a ridiculously low amount and barely profited from his creation, receiving only $500 per episode.

Hornberger also was unhappy with Alan Alda's portrayal of "Hawkeye" in the TV series, which he thought too liberal and anti-war, preferring Donald Sutherland's portrayal in the movie, feeling it was closer to his intent. *"My father was a political conservative"* his son William later said in an interview, *"he didn't write an anti-war book. It was a humorous account of his work, with serious parts thrown in about the awful kind of work it was, and how difficult and challenging it was."*

Hornberger, hospitalized for leukemia, passed away in Portland, Maine on November 4, 1997 at the age of 73. The novel remains in publication and the TV series continues to be broadcast as reruns worldwide.

SOURCES:

Blakemore, Erin. *Why the Real-Life Hawkeye Pierce hated M*A*S*H*
https://www.history.com/news/why-the-real-life-hawkeye-pierce-hated-mash

Evans, Tim. *Rowdy medical unit inspired M*A*S*H* USA Today, July 1, 2013

King, Maj. Booker and Jatoi, Co. Ismalil. *The Mobile Army Surgical Hospital (MASH): A Military and Surgical Legacy* Journal of the National Medical Association, May 2005

H. Richard Hornberger

Mifflin, Lawrie. *H. Richard Hornberger, 73, Surgeon Behind MASH* New York Times (Obituary) Nov. 7, 1997

Sherman, Dale. *M.A.S.H. FAQ: Everything Left to Know About the Best Care Anywhere* Hal Leonard Corporation (2016)

Forgotten No More

CHAPTER FIVE

LESLIE T. (AKA GEORGE A.) MAY
YOUNGEST KOREAN SILVER STAR

The Story is not unfamiliar. On October 9, 1950, as his unit was pinned down by intense enemy fire during the Battle of Kaesong, Corporal Leslie May crawled forward at great risk under fire to hurl hand grenades into enemy gun emplacements. What makes the story unique is that at the time of the action, Cpl. May was 15 years old.

Born in Wayne, Michigan on November 28, 1935, Leslie T. May used his brother George's birth certificate to fraudulently enlist in the US Army in 1948, (RA15260638) at the age of 13, and was sent to Japan as part of the post-WWII occupation forces, assigned to Company C, 1st Battalion, 8th Cavalry Regiment, 1st Cavalry Division.

When the North Korea invaded South Korea, the 8th Cavalry was initially ordered to make an amphibious landing at Inchon, but it was redirected to the southeastern coast of Korea at Pohang, a port 80 miles north of Pusan. On July 18, 1950 elements of the 8th Cavalry Division came ashore to successfully carry out the first amphibious landing of the Korean War.

The 8th Cavalry Regiment, reinforced by 1st Division artillery and other units, moved by rail, truck and jeep to relieve the 21st Infantry Regiment, 24th Division near Yongdong. By 22 July, all regiments were deployed in defensive positions as Typhoon Helene that pounded the Korean coastline.

The 1st Battalion, 8th Cavalry Regiment was deployed north of Taegu, now the temporary capital of South Korea and in the direct line of enemy advance. In the meantime, the 2nd Battalion held positions on the road from Maju to the southwest.

Forgotten No More

Their baptism of fire came on July 23 as the 8th Regiment was hit by heavy artillery fire and mortar barrage, and North Korean infantrymen swarmed toward their entrenched positions.

The next day, they suffered their first combat losses. For more than 50 days between mid-July and mid-September, in attack after attack, the 1st Cavalry Division and UN Forces performed the difficult, bloody task of holding the vital Pusan Perimeter.

The turning point came on September 15, when MacArthur unleashed his plan to get behind the advancing North Korean Army, Operation *Chromite*, an amphibious landing at Inchon, far behind the North Korean lines. The Inchon landing was an immediate success allowing the 1st Cavalry Division to break out of the perimeter and start fighting north.

The roads North were heavily mined and rather than taking the time to have the engineering battalion locate and dig up the mines, 17 tanks of "A" Company, 70th Tank Battalion were sacrificed to rapidly clear the mines along the routes.

From September 28 to October 3, the regiments were involved in mopping up operations of the large sector assigned to the 1st Cavalry Division. On 05 October 5, the 1st Cavalry Division advanced north of Seoul for the purpose of securing the US 1st Corps assembly area near the 38th Parallel. Led by I Company, the 5th Cavalry Regiment crossed to the north side of the Imjin River at Munsan-ni.

On October 7, the 16th Reconnaissance Company entered Kaesong, and that evening elements of the 1st Battalion, 8th Cavalry Regiment, arrived there. By the evening of October 8, the 7th and 8th Cavalry Regiments had secured the 1st Corps assembly area in the vicinity of Kaesong.

Some of the troops were within small arms range of the 38th Parallel, and on October 9, the 1st Cavalry Division crossed the 38th Parallel.

May, now a corporal, and a combat veteran at the age of 15, would earn a Silver Star Medal and Purple Heart for his actions at Kaesong. The citation for his Silver Star reads;

Leslie T. (AKA George A.) May

After Company C had been assigned the mission of crossing the 38th Parallel, the attacking elements were pinned down by a hail of automatic weapons and small arms fire, delivered by an enemy who occupied well-fortified positions and commanding terrain. Corporal May, an automatic rifleman, upon seeing his assistant squad leader killed while pointing out a good firing position, heedlessly moved forward, under scorching fire, to the designated spot where he began delivering effective counter fire on the North Koreans. When his weapon suddenly jammed, Corporal May dauntlessly picked up some grenades and crawled fearlessly toward the enemy emplacements. When within throwing distance, and under a stream of hostile fire which ripped and tore at the ground around him, Corporal May courageously hurled his grenade at the fanatic enemy until he was wounded.

May, in a newspaper interview late in November 1951 recalled; "*My squad leader got killed near Taejon, I jumped up and kept firing my rifle until it jammed. I threw three of my grenades, then grabbed two from another fellow and threw them. Then I got shot in the chest. Afterwards they counted 17 dead Koreans.*"

While in the hospital in Japan, his brother George learned of his wounds and petitioned the Army to discharge his younger brother as underage, since both parents were deceased.

In January 1951, after almost three years of service, 5 months on the front lines, May was honorably discharged as a corporal with the award of a Silver Star, Bronze Star and Purple Heart.

May returned to civilian life, but re-enlisted as a private shortly after his 17th birthday, this time under his own name. He was sent to Fort Bragg, North Carolina for airborne (paratrooper) training, then returned to Korea assigned to the 17th Infantry Regiment, 7th Infantry Division.

On April 17, 1953, May, once again a corporal was wounded by gunfire and treated for his wound. Again, on July 8. May, now a sergeant and squad leader, was wounded by gunfire, had his wound treated then returned to duty.

Explaining why he re-enlisted, May explained "*I got a factory job when I got out, but I didn't like it. Heck, by going back into the army I will be eligible to retire when I'm 34. "That ain't bad, and, besides,' I like it.*"

Forgotten No More

SOURCES:

Korean Vet, 13 Discharged as too young, to Re-enlist Waterloo Sunday
Courier, November 25, 1951

8th Cavalry Regiment, 1st Cavalry Division Association
https://1cda.org/history/history-8cav/

CHAPTER SIX

KURT CHEW-EEN LEE
Chinese-American at Sundong Gorge

The temperature was sub-zero, and a heavy snow was falling the night of November 2, 1950 as the lone figure moved forward in the darkness, somewhere in the vicinity of Sundong Gorge, North Korea.

Well forward of friendly lines, the small, slight Marine lieutenant was on a sole reconnaissance mission, occasionally firing his M-1 carbine or tossing a grenade to draw enemy fire and reveal the location of their positions. It was extremely hazardous work.

Often, as he drew near to their positions, he would yell out in Mandarin Chinese, *"Don't shoot. I'm Chinese"* and in their confusion he'd attack, firing into the position or tossing a grenade, sowing confusion among the Chinese troops. He had previously directed his machinegun platoon to target the enemy's muzzle flashes, with devastating effect.

For his actions that night and following morning, 1Lt. Kurt Chew-een Lee, the first Asian-American to be commissioned a regular officer in the US Marine Corps, would receive the Navy Cross, the nation's second highest award for valor.

Chew-een Lee was born in San Francisco, California on January 21, 1926, the third of seven children and the eldest of four sons of M. Yung Lee, a Chinese

Forgotten No More

immigrant who came to America from Guangzhou, China in 1920. He returned to China and brought back Gold Jade, his bride from an arranged marriage, around 1923. The couple had five children in five years.

Lee Sr. worked as a farm laborer, then bought a small farm, finally working as a labor contractor, supplying workers to local farms. It was during the Great Depression and when the farm failed, he moved the family to Sacramento where he operated a successful wholesale produce company supplying fruits and vegetables to hotels and restaurants.

Chew-een adopted the first name of Kurt, he later had it legally changed, and he grew up as an avid reader, primarily reading books on history and dreamed of becoming a fighter pilot in the US Army Air Corps (USAAC). He joined the Junior Reserve Officer Training Program (JROTC) at Sacramento High School where he graduated in June 1944.

Lee was attending Sacramento City College studying mining engineering when he was drafted on October 18, 1944. A physical revealed that Lee had a problem with depth perception, ending his dream of becoming a pilot and while he was waiting to be processed, he volunteered for the Marine Corps. *"I was told the Marines were the first in combat and the first to die"* he recalled. *"That was what I wanted."*

Asked to choose three preferences, Lee chose para-marine, tanks and sniper-scout. Instead, after taking basic training at Camp Pendleton, outside of San Diego, he was assigned to attend the language school to learn Japanese.

The majority of Lee's basic training unit was shipped to combat, most seeing action at Iwo Jima, while Lee was assigned as a language instructor, the only Asian in his class, with an accelerated promotion to sergeant. With the end of the war in August 1945, Lee applied for officer training.

After passing a four-year college equivalency test, Lee was accepted into the first post-war officer training class in September at the newly reinstated The Basic School (TBS) at the Philadelphia Navy Yard.

Kurt Chew Een Lee

Lee attended TBS from August 1945 to April 1946 when he was commissioned a second lieutenant, the first non-white and Asian American to be commissioned as a regular Marine officer. His first assignment was interrogating Japanese prisoners of war, first in Guam and later in China, after which he returned stateside.

At the start of the Korean War, First Lieutenant Lee was in command of the Machinegun Platoon, Company B, 1st Battalion, 7th Marine Regiment training at Camp Pendleton under Colonel Homer Litzenberg. The 7th Marines had reactivated on August 17 and was comprised of about 50/50 regulars and reservists called to active duty.

The regiment, commanded by Lt. Col. Raymond Davis, trained and resupplied from August 17-31 and embarked from San Diego for Korea on September 1 and arriving in Kobe, Japan on September 16.

Lee's first command of troops got off to a rocky start. Most of his men had never seen an Asian before and referred to him as "Chinaman" behind his back, but certainly never to his face. At 5'6 and 130 pounds, Lee was not an intimidating figure, and his men complained that he held almost constant classes and training during the two-week voyage, but his stern, no-nonsense demeanor garnered their respect, a respect that only increased once they were in combat.

The regiment landed at Inchon on September 21 and began driving North, forcing the North Koreans to retreat, and the South Korean capital of Seoul was liberated on September 27.

The 1st Marine Division, including the 7th Marines continued north, taking part in the Battle of the Hook (Oct. 2 – Oct. 28) advancing through snow-covered terrain in sub-zero temperatures. On October 30, the regiment was 6 miles north of Wonson when they received their first issue of cold weather gear.

At daylight on 26 October 1950 the First Marine Division began landing unopposed on the Kalma Pando peninsula, near Wonsan city, welcomed by the South Korean Army and their own Air Wing. Marine fighters had flown into Wonsan's airfield twelve days earlier and, supported by airlifted fuel, weapons and supplies, had been conducting combat flight operations against the North Koreans

The entire division was ashore by the end of October and after a period of mopping-up operations around Wonsan, headed north, to establish a base at Hungnam from which to strike inland toward Yudam-Ni near the Manchurian border. Unknown to the Marines, 10 divisions of Chinese "volunteers" had crossed the Yalu River into North Korea, beginning on October 14.

On November 2, Lee and his platoon were in the vicinity of Sudong Gorge. As Stanley Modrak, a radioman assigned to the 7th Marines recalled; *"We jumped-off early in the morning on October 31st. After a day-long trek climbing a narrow, dirt mountain road, Colonel Litzenberg picked a small valley just south of Sudong-ni to bivouac the regiment for the night. The rock-strewn valley was bordered by a dry stony riverbed and that was encircled by steeply-rising hills, climbing 1,000 to 1,500 feet higher, and dominating the valley floor."*

The night of November 2 was eerily quiet, and Lee remembered *"The Marines didn't know where the enemy was."* Moving forward of the lines, he took off on a solo reconnaissance hoping to draw enemy fire and instructing his men to target the enemy's muzzle flashes.

It was an extremely hazardous undertaking, but Lee later stated *"I never expected to survive the war so I was adamant that my death be honorable, be spectacular."*

As stated in Lee's Navy Cross citation:

"Immediately taking countermeasures when a numerically superior enemy force fiercely attacked his platoon and overran its left flank during the defense of strategic terrain commanding approaches to the main supply route south of Sudong, First Lieutenant Lee boldly exposed himself to intense hostile automatic weapons, grenade and sniper small-arms fire to carry out a personal reconnaissance, well in advance of his own lines, in order to re-deploy the machine-gun posts within the defensive perimeter.

Momentarily forced back by extremely heavy opposition, he quickly reorganized his unit and, instructing his men to cover his approach, bravely moved

up an enemy held slope in a deliberate attempt to draw fire and thereby disclose hostile troop positions."

Despite a serious wound to his knee, Lee continued leading his men until the Chinese retreated in confusion. He was wounded for a second time, in the right elbow from enemy sniper fire. Lee was evacuated to an Army MASH unit in Hamhung. For his actions at Sudong-ni, Lee was awarded the Navy Cross.

The Battle of Sudong-ni (Nov. 2-3) is considered the opening shots of the Chosin Reservoir Campaign and the first combat between US Marines and Communist Chinese troops in the Korean War.

After five days in the hospital, Lee learned that they were planning to evacuate him to a hospital in Japan. Unwilling to leave his men, Lee with his arm in a cast and sling, along with a Marine sergeant went AWOL and stole an Army jeep to return to their units at the front.

Dodging the M.P.s (Military Police), they ran out of gas and had to hike the last 10 miles. His company commander, although surprised by his return, immediately assigned him to take over the 2nd Rifle Platoon whose lieutenant had been injured and evacuated.

Forgotten No More

Despite his arm in a sling Lee continued to train the platoon whenever he had the opportunity. Lt. Lee was far from being finished fighting. On November 27, 67,000 Chinese troops overwhelmed a UN force of about 30,000 at the Chosin Reservoir, encircling the First Marine Division and elements of the Army's 7th Infantry Division.

Due to questionable leadership by X Corps commander, Major General Edward Almond, the force was strung out with its units unable to support each other. And there was only one road in and out.

Almond ordered the commander of the 1st Marine Division, Major General Oliver P. Smith, to begin a fighting withdrawl back towards the Hungnam.

On November 27, the 5th and 7th Marines attacked from their positions near Yudam-ni, on the west bank of the reservoir, with some success against the PLA forces in the area.

Over the next three days the 1st Marine Division successfully defended their positions at Yudam-ni and Hagaru-ri against Chinese human wave assaults.

On the night of December 2, Lee's 1/7th Marines, exhausted from lack of sleep after several days of fighting, was selected to break through and relieve Capt. William Barber's Fox Company, 2/7 Marines on Fox Hill, besieged and outnumbered, fighting to keep the Tonkton Pass, and the Chosin Reservoir road open.

The pass was critically important to the 5th and 7th Marines attempting to withdraw south from Yudam-Ni.

Lt. Col. Raymond Davis, 1st Battalion C.O., selected Baker Company to take the lead, followed by Able and Charlie Company. Lee's 2nd Platoon would spearhead the 500-man relief force. Leading from the front was Lt. Lee.

As Lee set out in darkness, in the middle of a blizzard, in knee-deep snow, Lee used only his compass to guide the way, leading 1st Battalion in single file, holding onto the man in front in limited visibility and sub-zero temperatures.

Carrying heavier loads as they moved up and down lightly wooded hills, through the extreme cold, Lee had no instructions from Davis on how to accomplish the mission except to stay off the roads with their heavily reinforced roadblocks. By this time, Lee had discarded the sling, but his arm was still in a cast, and his knee had difficulty supporting his weight on the uneven terrain.

Suddenly the column came under heavy fire from an adjacent rocky hill, and Lee directed the men to attack the hill with "marching fire" in which troops continue to advance as they apply just enough suppressive fire to keep the enemy's heads down.

When they reached the foot of the rocky hill, Lee and the battalion charged uphill, attacking the enemy in their foxholes. Lee, his right arm still in a cast, still managed to shoot two enemy soldiers on his way to the top. When he reached the top, he noticed that the other side of the hill was covered with enemy foxholes facing the other way.

The enemy had expected to engage the Marines coming up the road, but the foxholes were empty now as the enemy soldiers were running away, routed by 1st Battalion's attack from their rear.

As Lee's Silver Star citation would testify; "*Although sick and in a weakened condition from a previous combat wound, First Lieutenant Lee refused hospitalization and unflinchingly led his unit across trackless, frozen wastes of rocky mountain ridges toward a beleaguered Marine company. Through his indomitable spirit, he contributed materially to the success of the epic night march of his battalion which resulted in the relief of the isolated Marine unit and the securing of vital ground.*

On 2 December 1950 when the leading elements of his company were pinned down under intense enemy fire from a rocky hill mass, he skillfully maneuvered his platoon forward in an attack in the face of the heavy fire, personally accounting for two enemy dead and providing such aggressive and inspirational leadership that fire superiority was regained and the enemy was routed."

Following the rout, Lee was able to establish communication with Fox Company on Fox Hill. As 1st Battalion directed mortar fire against the enemy and called in an airstrike, Lee led Baker Company forward in an attack which forced a path to Fox Company. During this attack Lee took a bullet to the upper part of his right arm, above the cast on his elbow.

Lee continued to lead firefights against pockets of enemy soldiers in the Toktong Pass area until the road was secured.

On 8 December, Lee's platoon was attacking south on the main service road from Koto-ri when it was pinned down by heavy fire. Watching several Marines hit by enemy fire, Lee again exposed himself to enemy fire to move among his men, shouting encouragement and directing their withdrawal to covered positions.

Assured that the last of his wounded was under cover, Lee was seeking shelter when he was severely wounded by a burst of enemy machine gun fire. It was his last battle, being evacuated to Japan and ultimately stateside to recover from his wounds, and he was awarded a Silver Star for his actions. Both Captain Barber and Lt. Colonel Davis would be awarded the Medal of Honor for their part in the battle.

In 1962, Lee returned for a four-year assignment as an instructor at The Basic School, now at Quantico, Va. during the period from April 1962 until April 1965. Lee, now a captain, was initially assigned as the Commanding Officer of the Enlisted Instructor Company. When he was promoted to major on January 1, 1963, he was selected as the Chief, Platoon Tactics Instruction Group for 27 consecutive months.

He and his instructor staff of three majors and seven captains provided tactics instruction to a whole new generation of Marine Lieutenants and Warrant Officers and his former students include Generals Charles Krulak, a former Commandant and John Sheehan.

Lee served in the Vietnam War from 1965-66 with the 3rd Marine Division, III Marine Amphibious Force, as the Division Combat Intelligence Officer. He established the Division Document Translation Center for translating and processing of captured enemy documents for use by Marine units in the field, for which he was awarded the Marine Corps Commendation Medal with a combat "V" for valor.

Kurt Chew Een Lee

Lee retired as a major in 1968 and settled in Washington DC where he worked for the New York Life Insurance Company for seven years, then as a regulatory compliance coordinator for the National Rural Electric Cooperative Assn. until his retirement in 1995. He was married twice but had no children. Lee was active in veteran organizations, attended military reunions and traveled widely speaking about his military service.

Lee passed away on March 3, 2014 at the age of 88 and was buried in Section 55, #4970 of Arlington National Cemetery on September 30, 2014 with fully military honors including an honor guard from the Washington DC Marine Barracks and the "President's Own" Marine Band.

Two of his brothers, Chew-Fan and Chew-Mon, served as Army officers during the Korean War. Chew-Mon received the Distinguished Service Cross and rose to the rank of colonel, and Chew-Fan, a pacifist, served as a Medical Service lieutenant and a pharmacist who was awarded the Bronze Star.

In November 2002, General Davis, the former Assistant USMC Commandant, spoke at the Marines' Memorial about the Chosin Reservoir campaign. Davis, then a Lieutenant Colonel, commanding Lee's unit called Lee the bravest Marine he ever knew.

"He was very formal," his niece Lori Lee said. *"He was a really, really nice guy. But he was really proud to be a Marine. He was a Marine to the very end."*

SOURCES:

Clavin, Tom, Drury, Bob. The Last Stand of Fox Company: A True Story of U.S. Marines in Combat Grove/Atlantic Press (2009)

Davila, Robert. Obituary: Maj. Kurt Chew-Een Lee, 88, was Korean War hero Sacramento Bee (Ca) March 4, 2014

Forgotten No More

7TH Marine Regiment – Historical Diary- Aug. 1950-Dec. 1950
http://www.koreanwar2.org/kwp2/usmc/083/M083_CD22_1950_0
8_2281.pdf

Modrak, Stanley. Sudong- Ni- the Historic Clash as American Marines
meet Red Chinese Volunteers in the Korean War, Combat
Magazine, Volume 05 Number 04. Fall Oct 2007

Owen, Joseph R. Colder than Hell: A Marine Rifle Company at Chosin
Reservoir   naval Institute Press (2012)

CHAPTER SEVEN

MITCHELL RED CLOUD JR.
Lakota Warrior

Red Cloud was a war leader and Oglala Sioux chief best known for leading his people in several important victories over the forces of the United States Cavalry. He was strongly opposed to the westward expansion of the whites into Sioux lands and believed it was his mission to defend the Indians' last hunting grounds from intrusion by Whites taking the Bozeman trail to the Montana gold fields. Red Cloud made war on the United States.

Throughout 1867, not a single wagon moved along the trail to the goldfields. Finally, in 1868, the United States requested another peace council. In return for Red Cloud's pledge to live in peace, the government promised to abandon all forts along the trail and accept the territorial claims of the Sioux. Red signed the Treaty of Fort Laramie on November 6, 1868. This event is one of the few times when Indian military power compelled the United States to completely carry out the provisions of a peace treaty.

Red Cloud fought successfully against overwhelming odds and forced the United States to abide, at least temporarily, by the terms of their treaty and is remembered for his undaunted courage and fierceness in battle. Almost 42 years after his death, another Red Cloud would earn his place in the pantheon of American warriors.

This Red Cloud would also show undaunted courage in the face of overwhelming odds, this time with the United States Army in Korea, earning the Medal of Honor.

Mitchell Red Cloud Jr. was born on July 2, 1924 at Hatfield, Wisconsin, a member of the Ho-Chunk (Winnebago) nation. Some

Forgotten No More

sources cite 1925 as the year of his birth, but that seems unlikely since that would have made him 16 when he enlisted in the Marines.

Red Cloud was the eldest of three sons born to Mitchell Red Cloud Sr., a WW I Army veteran, and Lillian "Nellie" (Winneshiek) Red Cloud, a Ho-Chunk princess.

Growing up in rural America during the Depression, he learned to hunt and fish and enjoyed camping out, all skills that would serve him later in life. He was raised with stories of the Ho-Chunk warrior traditions and believed from an early age that a man who goes to war and dies for his nation lives forever.

He attended the Clay and Komensky Rural School, a one-room school house and the Winnebago Indian School, before dropping out of Black River Falls High School at age 16 hoping to enter the military. On August 14, 1941, shortly after his 17th birthday and with his father's permission, he enlisted in the United States Marine Corps.

Red Cloud was at Camp Elliott, San Diego Ca. when the Japanese attacked Pearl Harbor on December 7, 1941, and was initially assigned to 2nd Battalion, 9th Marines upon its reactivation on April 1, 1942 as part of the 2nd Marine Division.

On January 23, 1942 at the direction of President Franklin D. Roosevelt, Major General Thomas Holcomb, Commandant of the Marine Corps, authorized the formation of two Marine Raider Battalions to be used for special operations; the First Raider Bn. was formed on the east coast on February 16 under the command of Lt. Col. Merritt "Red Mike" Edson, and the Second Raider Battalion was formed three days later on the west coast under the command of Major Evans Carlson.

Mitchell Red Cloud, Jr.

On April 14, Red Cloud volunteered for, and was accepted into, the 2nd Raider Battalion, as his skills in hunting and camping was exactly the type of Marine that Carlson was looking to recruit. He was assigned to Weapons Platoon, Company F and in May, he sailed to Pearl Harbor, Hawaii as part of "Carlson's Raiders".

Carlson's 2d Raider Battalion boarded the submarines *Nautilus* (SS-168) under Cdr. William H. Brockman, Jr. and *Argonaut* (APS-1) under Cdr. John R. "Jack" Pierce, and raided Makin Island on August 17–18.

For his actions during the raid, Sergeant Clyde A. Thomason was posthumously awarded the Medal of Honor and was the first Marine recipient of this honor during World War II. Unfortunately, nine men were unintentionally left on the island when the Raiders returned to the submarines. These men were captured and later beheaded at Kwajalein.

On September 6, the entire battalion moved to Espiritu Santo in the New Hebrides Islands in preparation for deployment to Guadalcanal.

Pfc Red Cloud first saw combat during the Battle of Guadalcanal (August 7 1942 – February 9, 1943) in the Solomon Islands. On November 4, Red Cloud and his company disembarked from the destroyer USS *McKean* (DD-90) at Aola Bay,

Two days later, the battalion began the 28-day "Long Patrol" with the mission of silencing Japanese artillery firing on Henderson Field and mopping up scattered units of Japanese troops and finishing the mission on December 4, losing 19 killed and 122 wounded.

The Raiders successfully destroyed the enemy artillery and killed over 500 of the enemy, but fighting in Guadalcanal's extreme heat, the climate and tropical disease claimed more Raiders than did the Japanese, with 225 falling sick during their long patrol, including Red Cloud.

With his weight down to 75 pounds, and suffering from malaria, jaundice and malnutrition, Pfc Red Cloud was evacuated

Forgotten No More

stateside from Espiritu Santos on January 16, 1943 aboard the USS *Bellatrix* (AK-20) bound for San Diego.

Offered a medical discharge in February, Red Cloud declined, electing to remain on active duty. He wasn't through with the Japanese yet. Once he was fit for duty, Red Cloud requested reassignment to a combat unit and he was assigned to Weapons Platoon, Company A, 1st Battalion, 29th Marine Regiment, 6th Marine Division.

The First Battalion of the 29th Marine Regiment was formed as the Second Separate Infantry Battalion in February 1944 and re-designated as 1/29 while at sea on the way to its first combat assignment, attached to the Second Marine Division and saw its first combat on Saipan (June 15 – July 9, 1944)

Red Cloud was with the regiment when it made an uncontested landing on Okinawa on April 1, 1945, but 110,000 Japanese troops waited for the Marines in a system of fortified tunnels and bunkers on the southern tip of the island.

In fighting that has been described as "the costliest engagement in Marine Corps history, the 29th confronted a Japanese defensive line that stretched across the waist of the island from the Pacific Ocean to the South China Sea.

Following heavy fighting, the 6th Marine Division replaced the Army's 27th Infantry Division on the western side of the island. The 29th made steady progress south until May 12 when on the outskirts of Naha, Okinawa they ran into a low, loaf shaped hill (Asato-Ryokuchi) which was soon to be given the name "Sugar Loaf Hill". The hill was part of a complex of three hills that formed the western anchor of General Mitsuru Ushijima's Shuri Line defense.

On May 16, the 29th Marines relieved the 22nd Marines in the assault on Sugar Loaf Hill and in intense fighting, the 29th took heavy casualties, by some estimates two out of every three marines, making several frontal assaults before securing the hill on May 18. A day earlier, on May 17, Red Cloud took a gunshot wound to the left shoulder and evacuated to Guam.

Mitchell Red Cloud, Jr.

In the 10-day battle for Sugar Loaf Hill, the crest of the hill would change hands eleven times and result in 2,662 American casualties and the regiment being designated "combat ineffective" and withdrawn to Guam.

On November 9, 1945, Red Cloud, now a sergeant, was honorably discharged from the Marines with the award of two Purple Hearts.

Following his discharge, Red Cloud returned to Wisconsin where he visited relatives and married and had a daughter, Annita Red Cloud.

In December 1945, Red Cloud published an article in the *Wisconsin Archaeologist* about the surrender of Sauk leader Black Hawk to US authorities following the Black Hawk War. He also assisted Nancy Lurie, an anthropologist studying changes to Native American childcare over time.

In 1948, Red Cloud reenlisted, this time in the U. S. Army and was sent to Kyushu, Japan assigned to E Company, 2nd Battalion, 19th Infantry Regiment, 24th Infantry Division as part of the Army of Occupation.

The 24th Division was comprised of the 19th, 21st, and 34th infantry regiments, but the formations, due to the post-war drawdown and reduction in military spending, were undermanned and ill-equipped.

On June 25, 1950, 10 divisions of the North Korean People's Army (NKPA) launched an attack into the Republic of Korea in the south. President Truman was quick to respond.

On June 30, forward elements of the 24th Division, the ill-fated "Task Force Smith" comprised of 405 men of the 1st Battalion, 21st Regiment, a single, understrength infantry battalion, arrived in Korea by air with the rest of the division following by sea to land in Pusan. The 24th would be the first American troops to see combat in Korea. Red Cloud's battalion departed for Korea on July 3.

The 24th Infantry Division's mission was to slow the enemy advance and delay the advancing North Korean Peoples Army's

Forgotten No More

(NKPA) but it was repeatedly defeated and pushed further south by the NKPA's superior numbers and equipment, fighting in battles at or around Chochiwon, Chonan, Pyongtaek, Hadong and Yechon.

The division's 19th and 34th Regiments engaged the KPA 3rd and the 4th Infantry Divisions at the Kum River between July 13 and 16 and suffered 650 casualties of the 3,401 men committed there.

On July 19 and 20, the NKPA divisions attacked the 24th Infantry Division's headquarters in Taejon and overran it in the Battle of Taejon, losing 922 men killed and 228 wounded before withdrawing.

However, the 24th managed to delay the advancing North Koreans long enough for a large number of UN forces to arrive in Pusan and begin establishing defenses further south. By the time the 24th Infantry Division had retreated and reformed, the 1st Cavalry Division was in place behind it.

The 24th Division suffered over 3,600 casualties in the 17 days it fought alone against the NKPA 3rd and 4th Divisions. The 24th subsequently moved back to the Naktong River and was involved in the subsequent Pusan Perimeter campaign during August and September 1950.

During the First Battle of Naktong Bulge, (August 5-19), the 19th Infantry was moved up from reserve positions in to combat the NKPA 4th Division, which was attempting to break through their lines. In the subsequent Naktong Offensive, the 19th Infantry served as a reserve force to help units under attack in the Second Battle of Naktong Bulge (September 1-15).

On September 15 U.S. X Corps, with the 1st Marine Division in the lead, conducted an amphibious landing at Inchon, behind the NPKA lines. The U.S. Eighth Army began an offensive northward, breaking out of the Pusan Perimeter.

The 24th Infantry Division, with the Republic of Korea (ROK) 1st Infantry Division, moved to the left flank of the advancing Eighth Army, and moved north along Korea's west coast. In late October, however, as UN Forces approached the Yalu River,

Mitchell Red Cloud, Jr.

Chinese Communist Forces intervened in massive force on behalf of the faltering North Koreans.

By November, plans were being made for the withdrawal of all U.N. troops in North Korea to below the Chongchon River. The bridgehead across the river was to be protected in case the U.N. troops were ordered to resume offensive action.

On November 2, the north bank of the Chongchon River was held by the 27th British Commonwealth Brigade and the 19th Infantry Regiment. The two units were separated by a five-mile gap, supposedly patrolled constantly.

On November 5, the Chinese began probing the U.N. forces' defensive line, evading patrols and moving freely through the gap attempting to infiltrate to the rear. On that night, E Company, 2nd Battalion, 19th infantry was holding positions on Hill 123, near Chonghyon, just north of the river.

At approximately 3:20 a.m. in the frigid cold morning, under a full moon, 1,000 Chinese advanced to overrun E Company's position. Red Cloud, now a corporal, was manning a forward listening post in front of E Company's command post on the hill. His *"dauntless courage and gallant self-sacrifice"* would save his unit and result in the award of a Medal of Honor.

Red Cloud at 25, and a WW II combat vet, was highly regarded by the officers and men of his unit and he was remembered as *"a leader who was always good-hearted and kind towards the Korean people whom he was attempting to help,"*.

As Chinese soldiers charged from the brush not more than 100 feet away and, after sounding the alarm, Red Cloud jumped from his concealed position and opened fire at point-blank range with his Browning Automatic Rife (BAR) emptying magazine after magazine and *"delivered devastating pointblank automatic rifle fire into the advancing enemy."*

His intense and accurate fire slowed the enemy advance, allowing time for the company to withdraw and consolidate a defensive line. Despite two wounds and the death of the assistant

Forgotten No More

BAR man, Red Cloud "*...with utter fearlessness (he) maintained his firing position.*"

The 2nd Platoon Medic, Peter Woodley, came to Red Cloud's aid and applied field dressings to his wounds, but Red Cloud refused to be evacuated and Woodley moved on to assist others as he resumed firing.

Wound again, Red Cloud called for a medic and again Woodley responded and treated his wounds and again tried to evacuate Red Cloud, who again refused, asking for more ammunition and ordering Woodley to get the other wounded off the hill.

Woodley might have been the last man to see Red Cloud alive as he pulled himself to a standing position, and supporting himself on a tree, resumed fire as his company withdrew to fortified positions 1,000 yards south. Fatally wounded, his comrades retrieved his body the following morning surrounded by enemy dead. He'd been wounded eight times.

His actions are credited with "*alerting his company to the ambush and saving them from being overrun*".

On Tuesday, April 3, 1951 in a Pentagon ceremony, Gen. Omar Bradley, Chairman of the Joint Chiefs of Staff presented Red Cloud's mother, Nellie Red Cloud, with his posthumous Medal of Honor

Mitchell Red Cloud, Jr.

Nellie Red Cloud accepts her son's Medal of Honor April 3, 1951

Red Cloud was buried in the U.N. cemetery in Korea, but in 1955, his remains were returned to Wisconsin to be buried at Decorah Cemetery, on the grounds of the Ho-Chunk (Winnebago) Mission in Black River Falls, Jackson County.

The ceremony was a combination of Full Military Honors, Christian rites and Ho-Chunk traditions, and caught the notice of President Dwight Eisenhower who telegraphed *"I join with those who unite in tribute to the memory of Corporal Mitchell Red Cloud, Jr. His heroism has reflected lasting honor on the community which he loved and the country for which he gave his life"*

Forgotten No More

The entrance sign to the cemetery contains these words: "Burial Place of CPL. Mitchell Red Cloud Jr.

On Armed Forces Day, 18 May 1957, the United States Army named *Camp Red Cloud* in Korea in recognition of his actions.

On August 7, 1999, in a ceremony at the NASSCO shipyard in San Diego, California, the Navy christened the USNS *Red Cloud* (T-AKR-313), one of seven Strategic Sealift ships named in honor of Medal of Honor recipients.

Every July 4, the Ho-Chunk Nation observes Cpl. Mitchell Red Cloud Jr. Day. But perhaps his greatest tributes reside in the memories of those who remember him. As his daughter, Annita Red Cloud recalled

"I always say that I would have rather had a father than a Medal of Honor recipient or a war hero, but that's what I had in Mitchell Red Cloud Jr. He was killed ... defending his country and making freedom for the Korean people, which I'm very proud of."

SOURCES:

Baron, Scott. Valor of Many Stripes – Remarkable Americans in World War II McFarland Press (NC) 2019

Benner, Dana. Mitchell Red Cloud – Korean War Hero Military History Magazine, June 2006

Fisher, Franklin. Cpl. Mitchell Red Cloud Jr.
https://www.army.mil/article/138736/cpl_mitchell_red_cloud_jr

Rykken, Paul S. Corporal Red Cloud and the Power of Memory
http://brfhs.ss14.sharpschool.com/UserFiles/Servers/Server_7673
0/File/Rykken/APPush/REDCLOUDMEMORY.pdf

Sifuentes, Edward. Red Cloud was first to detect advancing enemy - San Diego (CA) Union Tribune, May 26, 2016

CHAPTER EIGHT

EMIL KAPAUN
"The Good Shepherd in Combat"

Chaplains have been a part of the United States military since July 29, 1775 when Gen. George Washington convinced the Continental Congress to authorize pay for one chaplain for each regiment of the Army, however the *first* chaplain was most likely William Emerson, who stood with the militia at the Battles of Lexington and Concord on April 19, 1775, praying for them and encouraging them in battle.

Since that time approximately 25,000 chaplains have provided religious and spiritual guidance to 25 million servicemembers and their families. It is one of the oldest branches of the US Army and they perform a variety of tasks in venues as diverse as service schools, military posts, hospitals and, when the nation requires it, on battlefields.

Of the 3,518 Medal of Honor recipients, nine have been awarded to chaplains for valor. Four during the Civil War; John Milton Whitehead, Grancis Bloodgood Hall, James Hill and Milton Lorenzo Haney. One from World War II, Lt. Cmdr Joseph Timothy O'Callahan and three from the Vietnam War; Captain Angelo J. Liteky, Major Charles Joseph Watters and, Lt. Vincent Robert Capodanno. One individual was awarded the Medal posthumously in 2016 by President Barack Obama.

Although unarmed, and considered non-combatants under the Geneva Convention, chaplains by the very nature of their calling operate near, and often on, the front lines. 400 chaplains have been killed in America's wars. The war in Korea was no exception.

Forgotten No More

1,600 chaplains saw service in Korea during the war and twelve of them would be killed in action, eight of those in the first few months of the war.

On July 16, 1950 during the Battle of Taejon, the 19th Infantry Regiment of the 24th Infantry Division was forced to withdraw or be overrun by advancing North Korean (NKPA) forces. 30 critically wounded soldiers were left behind under the care of a Medical Officer, Capt. Linton Buttrey, and a Chaplain, Capt. Herman Felholter, a Catholic priest who stayed with the wounded, guaranteeing certain capture. Both officers were unarmed and considered non-combatants, and both were wearing brassards denoting their status.

A patrol of the NKPA 3rd Division came upon the wounded men and, in what would become known as "The Chaplain-Medic Massacre" they murdered the unarmed men as they lay prone in stretchers, and Father Felholter as he prayed over the men. Capt. Buttrey escaped after being wounded. For his courage and dedication to his soldiers, Felholter was the first chaplain killed in the war and would be awarded a posthumous Distinguished Service Cross, the second highest award for valor.

Of the 12 chaplains killed during the Korean War, four would die while being held as Prisoners of War (POW) and one of those,

Capt. Emil Kaupen, would have his award of the DSC upgraded to the Medal of Honor in 2016, giving him the distinction of being the only chaplain awarded the Medal of Honor during the Korean War.

Emil Joseph Kapaun was born to Enos and Elizabeth (Hajek) Kapaun, Czech immigrants, in Pilsen, Kansas on April 20, 1916. He grew up with his brother Eugene on a farm three miles southwest of Pilsen and he graduated from Pilsen High School in May 1930. Kapaun

Emil Kapaun

also graduated from Conception Abbey seminary college in Conception, Missouri, in June 1936 and Kenrick Theological Seminary in St. Louis, Missouri, in June 1940.

On June 9, 1940, Kapaun was ordained a Catholic priest and he celebrated his first Mass at St. John Nepomucene Catholic Church in Pilsen. In January 1943, he was named Auxiliary Chaplain at Herington Army Airfield. In August of 1944, Kapaune entered the US Army Chaplains School at Ft. Devin, Massachusetts, graduating in October with a commission as second lieutenant in the Chaplain Corps.

Kapaun was assigned to Camp Wheeler, Ga. Where he and another chaplain ministered to 19,000 servicemen and women and their families.

In April 1945, he was sent to the China-India-Burma (CBI) theater of war, stationed in India.

His "parish" was over 2,000 miles in area which he serviced by jeep. He remained in India following the end of the war on September 2, 1945 and he was promoted to captain in January 1946.

Kapaun returned to the United States in May and was released from active duty in July 1946. He attended Catholic University of America in Washington DC under the G.I. Bill and graduated in February 1948 with a master's degree in education.

In September 1948, Kapaun returned to active duty and was sent to Ft. Bliss, outside El Paso, Texas and in December 1949, after taking leave to see his parents, for what would be the last time, Kapaun departed for Japan to join the occupation forces. Arriving at Mt. Fuji in January 1950, he was assigned to Headquarters, 8th Cavalry Regiment, 1st Cavalry Division.

On July 15, 1950, shortly after the outbreak of hostilities in Korea, the 1st Cavalry Division embarked from Tokyo Bay to Korea for the first amphibious landing at Inchon, with Kapaun going ashore at Po Hong Dong, Korea on July 18.

Forgotten No More

On August 2, 1950, near Kumchon, he rescued a wounded soldier despite intense enemy fire, heroism for which he would be awarded a Bronze Star Medal.

Late in August, Kapaun was assigned as chaplain to Headquarters Co. 3rd Battalion, 8th Cavalry Regiment, which saw fighting on the Pusan Perimeter. moving north in mid-September and the crossing the 38th Parallel into North Korea on October 9. The battalion advanced north to within 50 miles of the Chinese border.

During this time, Kapaun's only complaint was getting little sleep as he tirelessly ministered to the dead and dying, performed baptisms, heard confessions, offered holy communion and celebrated Mass, using the hood of his jeep as an improvised alter. Although he made it through battles unscathed, his jeep, trailer and Mass kit were frequent casualties of enemy fire.

Father Kapaun holding services October 7, 1950

During the Battle of Unsan (November 1-2), as Chinese Communist forces encircled the battalion, Kapaun moved fearlessly from foxhole to foxhole under direct enemy fire in order to provide comfort and reassurance to the outnumbered soldiers.

Emil Kapaun

According to witnesses, Kapaun, ignoring heavy enemy fire, raced into no man's land to drag wounded soldiers to safety. When he couldn't drag them, he dug shallow trenches to shield them from enemy fire.

Though the Americans successfully repelled the assault, they found themselves surrounded by approximately 20,000 of the enemy. Facing annihilation, the able-bodied men were ordered to evacuate. Kapaun, fully aware of his certain capture, rejected multiple opportunities for escape and elected to stay behind with the wounded.

After the enemy succeeded in breaking through the defense in the early morning hours of November 2, Kapaun continued to make his rounds even as hand-to-hand combat continued around him. He convinced an injured Chinese officer to negotiate the safe surrender of American forces.

Seeing a Chinese soldier about to execute a wounded GI, Kapaun *"with complete disregard for his personal safety and unwavering resolve, bravely pushed aside an enemy soldier preparing to execute Sergeant First Class Herbert A. Miller."* Hoisting Miller to his feet. Kapaun carried and supported Miller for several days as the prisoners marched north, until their column reached Pyoktong. Kapaun is credited for saving his, and numerous other lives.

Kapaun and the other prisoners were marched 87 miles to a temporary camp at Sombakol during the coldest winter in Korea in 100 years. Weak himself, he picked up soldiers who stumbled and encouraged those who had almost given up to keep moving, knowing that they would be shot if they couldn't keep up.

For the next seven months in the camps, first at Sombakul, and later Camp #5 at Pyoktong, Kapaun continuously risked his life to assist the weak, and to encourage and inspire the men. In the freezing temperatures, Kapaun offered fellow soldiers his own clothes. He risked being shot to sneak past guards to forage for food in the fields and convinced the POWs to share their meager rations with the weak, setting the example by sharing his own food.

Forgotten No More

With disregard for his own safety and comfort, he boiled water to purify the drinking water, risking punishment by building fires against guards' commands, as dysentery ravaged the men. He washed their clothes and cleansed their wounds, tended to the sick and wounded and dug latrines.

He also led prayers and spiritual services for the POWs, also at the risk of punishment. For his outspoken resistance, he earned brutal punishments from the guards, on one occasion being forced to sit outside naked in freezing temperatures, but Kapaun was revered by fellow POWs.

Kapaun developed a blood clot in his leg and his health began to deteriorate. Weak, he was nonetheless able to conduct forbidden Easter Service on March 25. When he fell ill, prison guards had him moved to the "hospital" which his comrades called a "death house" and he died on May 23, 1951 from dysentery and pneumonia and was buried in a mass grave.

Survivors of Pyoktong prison told stories of his courage, compassion, and spirit. They credited him with saving their lives, and hundreds more, before eventually succumbing to his own wounds and prison maltreatment.

On August 18, 1951, Kapaun was posthumously awarded the Distinguished Service Cross (DSC). He received this medal for *"tending to the wounded and dying without regard to his personal safety during the Battle of Unsan"*.

Sixty-three years later, on Thursday April 11, 2013, in a ceremony in the Oval Office, President Barack Obama would upgrade Kapaun's DSC and present his nephew, Ray Kapaun, with his posthumous Medal of Honor.

Emil Kapaun

In his remarks, President Obama stated, *"This is the valor we honor today, an American soldier who didn't fire a gun, but who wielded the mightiest weapon of all, a love for his brothers so pure that he is willing to die so that they might live."*

Perhaps, Obama summed it up best when he added *"That faith, that they might be delivered from evil, that they could make it home, was perhaps the greatest gift to those men. That even amidst such hardship and despair, there could be home ... that even in such hell, there could be a touch of the divine."*

Sources:

Chaplain (Capt.) Emil J. Kapaun – Medal of Honor
https://www.army.mil/medalofhonor/kapaun/

Hawkins, Kari. *History of service: Chaplains go where Soldiers go*
https://www.theredstonerocket.com/military_scene/article_
e963b32c-46e8-11e3-9ae4-001a4bcf887a.html

List of Korean War Medal of Honor recipients
https://en.wikipedia.org/wiki/List_of_Korean_War_Medal_of_Hono
r_recipients

Forgotten No More

CHAPTER NINE

THOMAS HUDNER
Faithful Wingman

A little after noon on December 4, 1950, a flight of six F4U *Corsairs* of Fighter Squadron 32 (VF-32) took off from the deck of the aircraft carrier USS *Leyte* (CV-32), part of Task Force 77 off the northwest coast of Korea in support of the 1st Marine Division's fighting withdrawal from the Chosin Reservoir.

The pilots were led by the squadron XO, Lt. Cmdr. Dick Cevoli and included Lt. George Hudson, Lieutenants junior grade Bill Koenig and Thomas Hudner and Ensigns Ralph McQueen and Jesse Brown, the first African American naval aviator.

It was a 100-mile flight from the Leyte to their target area on the west side of the reservoir, in the area of Yudam-ni and Hagaru-ni, flying in harsh, below freezing winter weather, seeking military installations, enemy troop concentrations, lines of communication or any other targets of opportunity.

The outcome of the mission would result in the award of the Medal of Honor to Lt. (jg) Hudner, the only Medal of Honor ever presented for crash landing an aircraft.

Born on August 31, 1924 in Fall River, Massachusetts, Thomas Jerome Hudner Jr. was the oldest of four sons and a daughter born to Thomas Sr. and Mary Hudner. His

Forgotten No More

father, of Irish descent, owned a chain of meat and grocery markets, Hudner's Markets.

In 1939, Hudner was admitted to Phillips Academy in Andover, Ma. about 15 miles north of Boston. Founded in 1778, it is one of the nation's oldest and most prestigious university prep schools whose graduates include 5 Nobel Prize Laureates and 6 recipients of the Medal

of Honor as well as his father, his uncle and eventually his three younger brothers. While at Phillips, Hudner competed in Track, Football, LaCrosse, and served on the student council.

Upon graduation in June 1943, in the midst of WW II, Hudner was appointed to the US Naval Academy by Representative Joseph W. Martin Jr., then the House minority leader. His classmates included James Stockdale, a fellow Medal of Honor recipient, Stansfield Turner, Admiral and CIA Director, and James Earl "Jimmy" Carter, future President of the United States.

After his graduation in June 1946, Ensign Hudner was assigned aboard the heavy cruiser USS *Helena* (CA-75) followed by a shore assignment as Communications Officer at the Naval Base, Pearl Harbor, Hawaii.

In 1948, developing an interest in aviation, Hudner applied for flight school. Accepted, he was sent to Naval Air Station (NAS) Pensacola, Florida for basic flight training, then to NAS Corpus Christi, Texas for advanced training.

In August 1949, Hudner qualified as a naval aviator and was issued his wings of gold and was assigned to VF-32, aboard the USS *Leyte*. He first met Jesse Brown when the two were assigned to the same 15-man squadron at the naval air station at Quonset Point, R.I.

The two first met while changing into their flight gear in a locker room. As Hudner recalled later, Brown didn't extend his hand, not wanting to embarrass him if he did not want to shake it. So, Hudner walked across the room and extended his. It was only a year after President Truman had ended segregation in the US Armed

Forces, but race relations and integration were not fully embraced or accepted by everyone.

It was an unusual friendship for the time, the privileged prep school student and the son of a Mississippi sharecropper, but they came to develop a mutual respect and friendship. Though technically junior in rank, Brown had logged more air time, and was therefore section leader with Hudner as his "tail end Charlie," flying at his rear.

VF-32 embarked from Norfolk, Virginia on two cruises to the Mediterranean aboard the *Leyte*, September 1949 to January 1950, and May to August 1950. In a demonstration of airpower, US aircraft flew over Beirut, Lebanon on August 13, supporting the Middle East against Communist pressure.

Leyte returned to Norfolk on August 24, and Hudner took leave to visit family and after 2 weeks of preparation, Leyte departed for Korea on September 6 to join Task Force 77 in the Far East supporting United Nations Forces in Korea.

Forgotten No More

Leyte arrived at the base for U.S. Fleet Activities in Sasebo, Japan on October 8, 1950 and made its final preparations for combat operations. From October 9 through January 19, 1951, the ship and her aircraft spent 92 days at sea and flew 3,933 sorties against North Korean and Chinese forces, targeting enemy positions, transportation, and communications.

Hudner and VF-32 flew missions targeting Wonson Harbor, Puckchong, Chonjin, and on December 4, the Chosin Reservoir to support the Marine's withdrawal.

After 45 minutes in the air, flying at about 6,000 feet, Brown's aircraft was hit by small-arms fire. Koenig radioed to Brown that he appeared to be trailing fuel. At least one bullet had ruptured a fuel line.

Brown, losing fuel pressure and increasingly unable to control the aircraft, and too low to bail out, dropped his external fuel tanks and rockets and attempted to land the craft in a snow-covered clearing on the side of a mountain.

Brown crash landed in a bowl-shaped valley near Somong-ni, 15 miles behind Chinese lines, and in freezing 15-degree weather.

The aircraft broke up upon impact and was destroyed. In the crash, Brown's leg was pinned beneath the fuselage of the Corsair, and he stripped off his helmet and gloves in an attempt to free himself, before waving to the other pilots, who were circling close overhead.

Others in his formation were sure that Brown had been killed on impact and Lt. Cmdr. Cervoli summoned a helicopter to collect his body. But when Hudner lowered his altitude and did a flyover to make sure, he was amazed at what he saw.

"I rubbed my eyes to make sure that I wasn't seeing things," he told Flight Journal in 2005. *"The canopy slowly rolled back, and Jesse waved at us!"*

As the flight surveyed the mountain for any sign of nearby Chinese troops, they received a signal that a rescue helicopter would come as soon as possible, but Brown's aircraft was smoking, and a fire had started near its internal fuel tanks.

The Marine rescue helicopter was still a half-hour away, but Hudner could see that smoke was rising from under the cowling, or engine casing, of the downed plane, and that Brown appeared stuck inside. If the fire didn't kill him, Hudner feared, the cold would. He resolved instantly to go in and rescue him. *"I was not going to leave him down there for the Chinese."* he later said.

On seeing that Ensign Brown was alive after his crash landing, Lieutenant Hudner jettisoned his rockets and all excess weight, and crash landed approximately 100 yards from Brown's wreck in two feet of snow. He found Brown conscious and calm, bareheaded, his fingers frozen, unable to reach his fallen gloves and helmet.

Hudner removed the woolen watch cap he had carried in his flight suit, placed it over Brown's head and wrapped his hands in an extra scarf. Looking into the cockpit he could see that Brown's right knee was crushed and jammed between the fuselage and the control panel.

Hudner could only use one hand because he needed the other to hold on to the plane and he was unable to free Brown. He radioed the incoming helicopter to bring an ax and a fire extinguisher.

Hudner attempted to pack the aircraft fire in snow and pull Brown from the aircraft but was not able to extract him as Brown began slipping in and out of consciousness, but in spite of being in great pain, did not complain to Hudner.

The rescue helicopter, a Marine Sikorski H03S, piloted by Lt. Charles Ward arrived around 3pm, but Hudner and Ward, were unable to put out the engine fire with a fire extinguisher. They tried in vain to free Brown with an axe for 45 minutes. They briefly considered, at Brown's request, amputating his trapped leg, but that wouldn't work because they had no firm footing due to the snow.

It was getting dark with the corresponding drop in temperature, and the helicopter, which was unable to operate in the darkness, was forced to depart with Hudner aboard, leaving Brown

Forgotten No More

behind. Hudner told Brown that he would return soon with better equipment.

"It was a bald-faced lie," Hudner would later say. He knew he could never get back in time. By the time Lieutenant Hudner left him, it is likely Brown might have already died from his injuries and exposure to the extreme cold. Before Brown lost consciousness for the last time, his last words, which he spoke to Hudner, were "*tell Daisy I love her.*"

Hudner sought permission to return to the wreck to help extract Brown, but his request was denied, as there was the fear of an ambush which could result in additional casualties.

On December 6, two days later, in order to prevent the body and the aircraft from falling into Chinese or North Korean hands, Brown's squadron returned to drench the crash site in napalm.

They recited the Lord's Prayer over the radio as they watched flames consume Brown's body. The remains of both Brown and the aircraft were never recovered. In 2013, Mr. Hudner returned to North Korea in hopes of retrieving the remains of Brown, but he was unsuccessful.

Brown was the first African American U.S. Navy officer killed in the war and was awarded the Distinguished Flying Cross posthumously. Hudner injured his back in the crash of his aircraft and was grounded for a month. He flew 27 combat missions, flying until January 20, 1951, when Leyte finished her rotation and returned to the Atlantic Fleet.

Hudner feared his actions might be punished, not celebrated, as his commanding officer had explicitly warned pilots against taking such risks. But Captain T.U. Sisson, captain of the *Leyte*, chose not to court-martial Hudner, summarizing his feat this way: *"There's been no finer act of unselfish heroism in military history."*

On April 13, 1951, in a ceremony in the Rose Garden of the White House, President Truman awarded Hudner the Medal of Honor for "exceptionally valiant action and selfless devotion to a shipmate" and telling him *"I'd much rather have received this medal than be elected the president."* Hudner's was the first of seven Navy Medals of Honor in the Korean War and 1 of 11 Medals of Honor awarded for the Battle of Chosin Reservoir.

Also present at the ceremony was Daisy P. Brown, Ensign Brown's widow and the two began a friendship that would extend 50 years.

When questioned by the press about his act when he received the Medal of Honor from Pres. Harry S. Truman, Hudner spoke simply, but his words had particular weight in a time of segregation. *"Jesse would have done the same for me,"*

Hudner remained in the Navy for another 22 years. After receiving the Medal of Honor, Hudner served as a flight instructor at NAS Corpus Christi, 1952-1953, then as a staff officer for Carrier Division 3, in Japan, 1953-1954. In 1955 and 1956, he served in Air Development Squadron 3 at NAS Atlantic City, New Jersey, where he flew developmental and experimental aircraft, primarily jet engine-powered aircraft.

Forgotten No More

In October 1957, Hudner served in an exchange program with the U.S. Air Force, flying for two years with the 60th Fighter-Interceptor Squadron at Otis Air Force Base flying the F-94 *Starfire* and the F-101 *Voodoo*. Promoted to commander, in 1959 he served as aide to the Chief of the Bureau of Naval Weapons until 1962, when he attended the Air War College at Maxwell AFB in Montgomery, Alabama.

Upon graduating in July 1963, he returned to flying duty and was appointed the executive officer of Fighter Squadron 53 (VF-53), flying the F-8E *Crusader* aboard the attack carrier USS *Ticonderoga.* (CVA-14)

After serving as the XO, Hudner assumed command of VF-53, after which he was assigned as Leadership Training Officer at the office of Commander, Naval Air Forces, at NAS North Island in Coronado, Ca.

Hudner was promoted to captain in 1965, taking command of Training Squadron 24 at NAS Chase Field, Texas, which he commanded until 1966.

In 1966 Hudner shipped out to his second war, assigned to USS *Kitty Hawk*, (CVA-63) first as a navigator, then as the ship's executive officer. *Kitty Hawk* deployed to South Vietnam 1966-1967, launching missions in support of the Vietnam War. Hudner saw no combat and flew no missions himself.

Hudner's final Navy posting was as the head of Aviation Technical Training in the Office of the Chief of Naval Operations in Washington, D.C., where he remained until his retirement. Hudner retired as a Captain in February 1973 after 27 years of service. In addition to his Medal of Honor, his awards include the Legion of Merit, Bronze Star and Air Medal.

Thomas Hudner

After his retirement, Hudner worked as a private consultant, and later worked with the United Service Organizations (USO). Because of his Medal of Honor, he was honored by numerous veteran's groups. From 1991 to 1999, he served as Commissioner for the Massachusetts Department of Veterans' Services.

Hudner died at his home in Concord, Massachusetts, on November 13, 2017, at the age of 93. On April 4, 2018, Hudner was interred in Section 54, Grave 2135 at Arlington National Cemetery with full military honors.

The ceremony attended by General Joseph Dunford, Chairman of the Joint Chiefs of Staff and Admiral John Richardson, the Chief of Naval Operations, included a "missing man formation" flyover by Strike Fighter Squadron 32 (VFA-32).

Cmdr. Nathan Scherry, Commanding Officer of the soon to be commissioned destroyer named in Hudner's honor eulogized him, saying *"A hero the day he tried to rescue Jesse, a hero when he served our community and a hero when he passed."* At his passing, Hudner was the last living recipient of the Medal of Honor from the Korean War.

On December 1, 2018, the USS *Thomas Hudner* (DDG 116), an Arliegh Burke Class Destroyer was commissioned in Boston.

SOURCES:

Capt. Thomas J. Hudner, Jr., Korean War Medal of Honor Recipient, Passes Away - Naval History and Heritage Command https://www.history.navy.mil/news-and events/news/2017/november/Thomas_Hudner_Passes.html

Margolick, David. *Thomas Hudner, War Hero in a Civil Rights Milestone, Dies at 93* New York Times (NY) Nov. 13, 2017

Makos, Adam. *Devotion: An Epic Story of Heroism, Friendship, and Sacrifice* Ballantine Books, NY (2017)

Forgotten No More

CHAPTER TEN

THE McGOVERN BROTHERS
A Brother's Sacrifice and a Father's Stand

"From now until the end of the world, we and it shall be remembered. We few, we Band of Brothers. For he who sheds his blood with me shall be my brother."

William Shakespeare ("Quote from King Henry V")

Since the dawn of time, brothers have gone to war. Sometimes they fought each other, like in the American Civil War, oftentimes called "The Brother's War". Sometimes they fought together on the same side, like the ten Calpin Brothers during WW I. And occasionally, they perished together, like the five Sullivan brothers aboard the USS Juneau during WW II. The Korean War would prove no different.

Robert M. and Jerome F. McGovern were brothers born in Washington D.C., Robert on January 24, 1928 and Jerome on October 4, 1929. They grew up together, went to school together, went to war in Korea together, died leading men in battle within 11 days of each other and came home together to be buried at Arlington National Cemetery together and both would be recognized for their valor. But the award of the Medal of Honor would spark controversy from an unexpected source.

John Halsey and Marguerite Warner McGovern would raise a family of six children, four boys and two girls, in the Petworth section of Washington D.C. John was the oldest, born in 1925 and was three years Robert's senior. Sister Margaret Jane was a year older than Robert, and then (Francis) Jerome, who was called Jerome, and was little more than a year younger. Brother Charles and sister Elizabeth completed the large and close-knit family. Robert and Jerome, due to the closeness of age, were especially close.

Family values included honesty, hard work, charity, and a good education. To that end, the McGovern children attended St. Gabriel's Grade School and later, St. John's College High School.

In 1942, the same year older brother John enlisted in the Army Air Force, Robert enrolled at St. John's College High School which was established in 1851 and is the second oldest Christian Brothers School in the United States Its Cadet Corps is the oldest Army JROTC program in the country. Jerome followed him, two years behind. Both brothers joined the Corps of Cadets.

John served during WW II as a flight engineer aboard B-24 Liberators in the Pacific theater of operations and returned home safely at the end of the war.

In June 1946, Robert graduated St. John's and enlisted in the US Army and in 1947 he was accepted for Officers Candidate School (OCS) at Ft. Benning, Georgia. Upon graduating, he was commissioned a second lieutenant and sent to airborne school before being assigned to the 187th Infantry Regiment, 11th Airborne Division. He joined the regiment at Camp Crawford, Hakaido Island, Japan as part of the occupation forces. While in Japan, he assisted Franciscan Missionary nuns in raising funds and supplies to assist orphaned and abandoned children from family and friends in the States.

The McGovern Brothers

In April 1949, the regiment returned to the United States and was stationed at Camp Campbell, Kentucky. Re-designated the 187th Airborne Infantry Regiment on June 30, 1949, it remained assigned to the 11th Airborne Division. In early 1950, the 187th participated in "Operation Swarmer," the largest peacetime airborne maneuver in history.

On 1 August 1, 1950, responding to the crisis in Korea, the regiment became the 187th Airborne Regimental Combat Team (ARCT) when supporting units were added, and it deployed back to Japan, arriving on 20 September 1950.

Like his brother, Jerome enlisted in the Army after graduating St. John's in 1948, and after basic training at Ft. Riley, Kansas, he attended OCS at Ft. Benning, was commissioned a second lieutenant and graduated the Basic Airborne Course, earning the jump wings of a paratrooper. In the summer of 1950, Jerome joined his brother in Japan, also assigned to the 187th ARCT.

After hostilities broke out in June, the advance party of the 3rd Battalion, 187th ARCT, including both McGovern brothers, arrived in Korea, parachuting into Kimpo Airfield on September23, arriving almost a week after MacArthur's surprise landing at Inchon on September 17.

Forgotten No More

JEROME (L) and ROBERT (R) MCGOVERN

One month later, on October 20, 1950, the regiment made successful combat parachute assaults near the towns of Sukchon and Sunchon in North Korea as part of the Battle of Yongju.

The purpose of that drop was to capture members of the North Korean Government fleeing Pyongyang and also to liberate American POWs being moved from Pyongyang toward the Manchurian border. Neither objective was realized.

In November, with a shortage of officers due to a high casualty rate, both brothers were reassigned out of the 197th. Robert was sent to Company A, 1st Battalion, 5th Cavalry Regiment 1st Cavalry Division, and Jerome to first Headquarters Company, then Company I, 3rd Battalion, 9th Infantry Regiment, 2nd Infantry Division. Both brothers saw their share of combat as the new year approached.

Following the withdrawal of UN forces following On the night of November 25, 1950, in the Battle of the Ch'ongch'on River (Nov.25-Dec.2) Communists launched a series of surprise attacks

The McGovern Brothers

along the Ch'ongch'on River Valley at the western half of the Second Phase Offensive, effectively destroying the Eighth United States Army's right flank while allowing PVA forces to move rapidly into UN rear areas.

In the subsequent battles and withdrawals during the period of November 26 to December 2, 1950, the US Eighth Army managed to avoid being surrounded by PVA forces, but the PVA 13th Army was still able to inflict heavy losses on the retreating UN forces. In the aftermath of the battle, the US Eighth Army's heavy losses forced all UN forces to retreat from North Korea to the 38th Parallel.

On December 31, the Communists began their Third Phase Offensive, also known as the Third Battle of Seoul or the Chinese Year Near Offensive, as China's Chairman Mao Zedong ordered the Chinese People's Volunteer Army to cross the 38th Parallel in an effort to pressure the UN forces to withdraw from South Korea.

The Chinese 13th Army attacked the Republic of Korea Army (ROK)'s 1st, 2nd, 5th and 6th Infantry Divisions along the 38th Parallel, breaking through the UN defenses at the Imjin River, Hantan River, Gapyeong and Chuncheon. To prevent the PVA forces from overwhelming the defenders, the US Eighth Army, now under the command of Lieutenant General Matthew B. Ridgway, appointed its new commander on December 23, ordered the evacuation Seoul on January 3, 1951.

Although PVA forces captured Seoul, Chinese supply lines were stretched to the breaking point, and by the end of the battle, the Chinese invasion of South Korea roused UN support for South Korea, and the idea of evacuation was abandoned by the UN.

Ridgway revitalized the 8th Army, extorting his troops to "Find Them, Fix Them, Fight Them, Finish Them". On January 15, 1951 he instituted a reconnaissance in force, Operation Wolfhound, followed by Operation Thunderbolt, a full-blown counter-offensive on January 25.

It was the coldest winter in 100 years with sub-zero temperatures and relentless snow Americans were inadequately equipped as they nonetheless advanced, capturing ridge after ridge. As Pvt. Ted White an African-American soldier in the 24th Infantry Rgt. would later recall in Rudy Tomedi's book, No Bugles, No Drums, "We went out every day and we attacked. Seems like that's all we did was attack. We hardly ate. We hardly slept. We just attacked."

In late January, the 8th Cavalry met with resistance at Yangji-ni, slowing forward progress and the 5th Cavalry was ordered to go around the 8th and seize Hill 312, five miles from Kimnyangjang-ni. It was desperate hand to hand combat between the troopers of the 1st Battalion, 5th Cavalry and the strongly dug in Chinese.

As Alpha Company's commander, Capt. Richard Wolf, later wrote in a letter to Halsey McGovern "The Chinese had broken contact with us and it was our job to go out and find them and see how badly they wanted to fight."

On January 29, "Charlie" Company was ordered to dislodge the Chinese troops on Hill 312 and took heavy casualties in an unsuccessful daylong assault. The following day, A and B Companies were ordered to take the hill. On the morning of January 30, under cover of a dense fog, Robert McGovern led his platoon up the steep slope for over three hours to advance to within 75 yards of the summit when the fog lifted.

As the 1st Cavalry Division history recorded, "For a time, the outcome hung in the balance, then the third platoon, "A" Company came charging up the hill with fixed bayonets."

The Chinese were in a series of fortified emplacements and began raining down heavy machinegun and small-arms fire on the advancing Americans. As his Medal of Honor citation would describe it,

"As 1st Lt. McGovern led his platoon up a slope to engage hostile troops entrenched in bunker-type pillboxes with connecting trenches, the unit came under heavy machine gun and rifle fire from the crest of the hill, approximately 75 yards distant. Despite a wound sustained in this initial burst of withering fire, 1st Lt. McGovern, assured the men of his ability to continue on and urged them forward. Forging up the rocky incline, he fearlessly led the platoon to within several yards of its objective when the ruthless foe threw and rolled a vicious barrage of hand grenades on the group and halted the advance. Enemy fire increased in volume and intensity and 1st Lt. McGovern realizing that casualties were rapidly increasing and the morale of his men badly shaken, hurled back several grenades before they exploded. Then, disregarding his painful wound and weakened condition he charged a machine gun emplacement which was raking his position with flanking fire. When he was within 10 yards of the position a burst of fire ripped the carbine from his hands, but, undaunted, he continued his lone-man assault and, firing his pistol and throwing grenades, killed 7 hostile soldiers before falling mortally wounded in front of the gun he had silenced."

Behind him, Robert's soldiers looked on in horror as numerous enemy soldiers overwhelmed their lieutenant and watched as bullets riddled his body. The courage of this lone, one-man assault inspired his men and, determined to avenge his loss, they fixed bayonets and, throwing grenades, they "charged with such ferocity that hostile positions were overrun and the enemy routed from the hill."

Capt. Hunt helped other soldiers carry their lieutenant down off Hill 312. Remembering the day, Hunt would write "Bob McGovern went up ahead and he saw where most of the enemy was, and he threw himself into the trench and wiped them out." It was his men that would lobby for his Medal of Honor.

But there were other ridges yet to be taken. In early February, 2Lt. Jerome McGovern's platoon was in the vicinity of Kumwang-ni, about 15 miles north of where his brother was killed. The 9th Infantry took heavy casualties as they advanced. Pvt. Joseph Lovetro, a soldier in Company I recalled "We were getting knocked off so fast. It was a slaughterhouse."

Unaware that his brother had been killed, Jerome wrote home to his parents "The company commander has said something is going to break in the next day or two, so I am going to turn in early so I will be prepared for any eventuality. I hope it is good."

Forgotten No More

On the night of February 10, I Company attacked Chinese troops dug into fortified positions atop Hill 442. Advancing approximately 300 yards, Company I came under attack from intense mortar, automatic weapons and small arms fire. Ignoring a wound he had received, 2Lt. McGovern reorganized his platoon and resumed the assault.

In pain and weak from his wound, he led his men up the hill, much as his brother had done, and his platoon followed him in a fierce charge upon the Chinese positions. He was the first to reach the crest of the hill, and while urging his men forward, he was wounded a second time, this time mortally, but like on 312, his platoon took their objective, routing the Chinese. In the heat of battle, his body was overlooked, and Jerome was reported Missing in Action (MIA) on March 3.

On February 12, 1951, Halsey McGovern had received a telegram advising the family that Robert had been killed in action and he wrote a letter to Jerome three days later to break the news that his brother was dead, only to have the letter returned, marked "Missing in Action". It wasn't until June that he learned of Jerome's death.

The McGovern brother's funeral on November 15 was a major event in Washington DC, held at St. Gabriel's Church where both boys had been baptized, made their first Holy Communion, and were confirmed, and presided over by Bishop John McNamara. Hundreds attended, including the St. John's Cadet Corps and numerous national newspapers.

In his eulogy, McNamara said "I am reminded of a lesson that was written deep in their hearts. He who loves God is a Christian; he who loves his country is a patriot. But he can be neither, who is wanting in the spirit of sacrifice."

The McGovern Brothers

Accompanied by a military honor guard, their flag draped coffins crossed the Potomac River to Arlington National Cemetery to be buried, side by side, with full military honors.

Two months later, the Army's plan to award a posthumous Medal of Honor to Robert and the Silver Star to Jerome met resistance from an unexpected source and created a national controversy when Halsey McGovern, their father, announced his intention to refuse the awards.

It was the first time in history that the nation's highest decoration for valor had ever been turned down. Astonished Defense Department officials said the citations and medals would go into the dead soldier's files anyway.

The elder McGovern stated that politics had nothing to do with his decision. "I don't like the general idea of these so-called awards anyhow… I don't like the idea of singling out a few men for medals when thousands of other soldiers are dying too. They give everything they've got. Take for example a boy who gets ambushed

Forgotten No More

alone. Chances are he will never get any awards. Whoever is left behind might think he didn't measure up."

But he also expressed a growing sentiment about the war, a sentiment that would be repeated a decade later in Vietnam. McGovern felt Truman's Far East policies had led to the Korean war and that men in combat were not given enough military support. McGovern himself, when asked what he disliked about Truman, said: "His record."

"Truman's failure to put an all-out war effort behind US soldiers in Korea sears the soul of an understanding father" he wrote to the Army in turning down the Medal of Honor and Silver Star.

McGovern lived to be 97 and never changed his views. In 1990, seven years after his death, the surviving McGovern siblings asked the Army to issue the medals, and they were presented to St. John's, where they are displayed to commemorate the McGoverns' valor and sacrifice.

For Halsey McGovern, his sons' sacrifice is best expressed in the words inscribed on their shared headstone: "To their conscience they were true. And had the genius to be men."

Sources:

Avramovic, Ivana. *Brother visits camp named for war hero*, Stars and Stripes - October 23, 2003

Blasting Truman, Dad of 2 Slain Heroes Spurns Medal of Honor Daily News, New York (NY) January 12, 1952

Francis Jerome McGovern – Arlington National Cemetery website; http://www.arlingtoncemetery.net/jfmcgove.htm

Sterner, C. Douglas. *The McGovern Brothers* Home of Heroes website https://homeofheroes.com/heroes-stories/korean-war/the-mcgovern-brothers/

The McGovern Brothers

Vogel, Steve. *Fallen Sons and One Father's Stand,* Washington Post,
    May 28, 2000

CHAPTER ELEVEN

HIROSHI MIYAMURA
First Top-Secret award of the Medal of Honor

On August 23, 1953, 20 weary P.O.W.'s (Prisoner of War) boarded a Soviet truck and were driven to Panmunjon, near the North Korean DMZ, where they crossed over Freedom Bridge and boarded ambulances for the ride to the village of Taesung, also known as "Freedom Village," the only South Korean settlement in the 160-mile long and 2.5 mile-wide demilitarized zone (DMZ) that divided, and still divides North and South Korea.

The men, former prisoners of the North Koreans, who were suffering from dysentery, the effects of inadequate food and shelter, constant harassment and in some case torture, were mostly jubilant at finally being released. They traded their faded blue prison uniforms for oversized fatigues, were examined by doctors, nurses and medics, and debriefed by Intelligence officers

One of the former POWs, a slight Japanese-American corporal who had endured more than his share of abuse from his North Korean captors, stood quietly apprehensive. At the time of his release, he was emaciated, weighing just 100 pounds, his

Forgotten No More

newly issued uniform hanging on him after losing almost 50 pounds in 28 months of captivity.

As he stood waiting, he was shocked to hear someone call out "Are you Corporal Hiroshi H. Miyamura?" The soldier turned to see a United States Army captain regarding him. "Are you Corporal Hiroshi H. Miyamura?" he repeated.

Stunned, Miyamura could only numbly nod. The man said" Come with me" and escorted him to a room where Brigadier General Ralph Osbourne, the base commander, waited with a room full of reporters.

As Miyamura recalled in a 2001 interview "*We crossed Freedom Village. To this day I don't remember crossing the bridge. All I can remember is seeing a big U.S. flag flying in the breeze, and I just concentrated on that flag. After a short period of relaxation, I was escorted to a room where I met a reporter from my hometown and the general of the 3rd Infantry Division.*"

Gen. Osbourne addressed the reporters "*Gentlemen of the Press, I want to take this occasion to welcome the greatest V.I.P., the most distinguished guest to pass through Freedom Village. Sergeant Miyamura, it is my pleasure to inform you that you have been awarded the Medal of Honor.*"

Learning that he would receive the Medal of Honor, he modestly recalled "*I didn't feel I was doing anything out of the ordinary. I felt I was doing my job.*" It was also when he first learned that he'd been promoted to sergeant and awarded the Purple Heart.

His Medal of Honor citation, dated December 21, 1951, had been filed away and classified "top-secret" until the start of Operation Big Switch, the exchange of POWs between the United Nations command and the Communists, when it was delivered to U.S. Eighth Army headquarters shortly after the Korean armistice was signed in late July 1953.

One of seven children (Sources differ as to whether its six or seven) of Japanese immigrants, Hiroshi Miyamura was born in Gallup, New Mexico on October 6, 1925.

His parents immigrated from Kyushu, Japan and settled in Gallup around 1906. Except for his older sister who was born in

Japan, his other four sisters and a brother were all born in or near Gallup. Yaichi and his wife opened the OK Café in Gallup, off of the legendary Route 66 in 1923.

Gallup was a rowdy railroad town, filled with bars and cathouses, frequented by miners, cowboys and railroad workers, with a population of 7,000 with a diverse blend of ethnicities, including Russians, Finns, Slavs, Italians, Mexicans, Navajos, Zunis and a community of about 25 Japanese families.

Miyamura and his siblings grew up speaking English, and never considered themselves anything but American. Although the community was fully integrated, discrimination wasn't unknown, and Miyamura took up boxing and joined ROTC in high school. He was given the nickname "Hershey"

Following the Japanese attack on the naval base at Pearl Harbor, Territory of Hawaii on December 7, 1941, President Franklyn Delano Roosevelt subsequently signed Executive Order 9066 on February 19, 1942 which authorized the removal of any or all people from military areas "as deemed necessary or desirable."

The military in turn defined the entire West Coast, home to the majority of Americans of Japanese ancestry, as a "Coastal Military Zone' and ordered more than 120,000 West Coast Japanese, 60% of whom were American citizens, to be relocated to remote internment camps. It is worth noting that no German-Americans or Italian-Americans were interned.

Relocation was not mandatory for communities outside the military zone and local authorities were given discretion as how to proceed. Unlike nearby communities like Clovis, New Mexico and Winslow, Arizona, Gallup left its Japanese citizens undisturbed. As Sheriff Dominic "Mickey" Mollica stated, *They are citizens and we are not going to round them up.* But Miyamura would see sad Japanese faces peering out train windows as they passed through Gallup.

Hershey graduated from Gallup High School in June 1943 and immediately he tried to enlist in the Army. He was rejected as an enemy alien, but as the need for additional troops became more acute, the policy was revoked, Miyamura was drafted into the army

Forgotten No More

on February 29, 1944 and took basic training at Camp Blanding, Florida.

He was next sent to Camp Shelby, Mississippi and assigned to Company D of the 100th Infantry Regiment, 442 Regimental Combat Team (RCT) as a machine gunner. Initially denied duty overseas because of his young age, he was eventually sent overseas, and rejoined the 442nd in Naples, Italy, but saw no combat. Five days after he arrived, the war in Europe was over with the German surrender on May 8, 1945.

After brief duty as occupation troops, Miyamura and the 442nd returned to the United States as national heroes. On July 15, 1946, in a ceremony on the White House south lawn, President Harry Truman reviewed the 442nd RCT following a parade down Constitution Avenue.

It was raining hard but when aides suggested that the President might want to cancel, Truman is said to have replied, *"Hell no, for what these boys have done, I can stand a little rain"*. He told the 442nd *"You fought the enemy abroad and prejudice at home, and you won"*.

Miyamura was honorably discharged from the Army on July 18, 1946 and promptly enlisted in the Army Reserve for a three-year term. He attended the Milwaukee School of Engineering in 1947 and married Tsuroko "Terry" Tsuchimori in June 1948. They would have three children together.

Miyamura re-enlisted for another three years in the Reserves in June 1949 and was called to active duty on September 21, 1950 shortly after the Korean War started. After nine weeks of refresher training, he was flown to Japan where he joined H Company, 2nd Battalion, 7th Infantry Regiment, 3rd Infantry Division, assigned as a squad leader of a machine squad.

The 7th Regiment embarked from Japan and landed at Wonsan on the eastern coast of Korea on November 21, 1950. Joined with the 15th and 65th Infantry, it moved to the northwest of the Hungnam area where it covered the withdrawal of American soldiers and Marines from the Chosin Reservoir maintaining a pathway south to the port of Hungham.

Hiroshi Miyamura

The 7th Regiment was the last unit off of Pink Beach at Hungnam and withdrew by sea on December 24, 1950. Transported to Pusan, the regiment completed unloading on December 30 and moved north to Kyongju after being refitted with new gear. The regiment was put into the defensive line north of Seoul.

On the night of April 22, 1951, Gen. Peng Dehuai, commander of the Chinese Peoples Volunteers (CPV) launched the Fifth Phase Offensive, or Spring Offensive, the largest offensive to date, with 700,000 troops smashing through the 6th ROK Division, and creating a hole in the United Nations (UN) force's lines between the 24th Division to the west and the 1st Marine Division to the east.

Elements of the Ninth and Thirteenth CPV Army Corps poured through the gap in overwhelming numbers. On the night of April 24, Cpl. Miyamura and Company H was occupying a defensive position near Taejon-ni, Korea, when the enemy attacked with a large force, threatening to overrun the position.

Miyamura listened as Red Chinese bugles howled, and whistles shrieked. *"It seemed like there were just thousands of ants marching across the frozen river toward us"* he would later recall in a speech in 2010.

The 3rd Division was ordered to pull back. H Company withdrew under a heavy enemy mortar barrage followed by two separate battalion-size probes. But the word never reached Miyamura's position.

Miyamura, positioned between a light and a heavy machine gun, directed their fire on the advancing Chinese. Shortly before midnight, the Chinese again advanced up the slope. He called out to his gunners, ``Short bursts, short bursts!'' as he fired off short bursts from his M-1 carbine and hurling grenades down the slope. The attack was finally stopped.

Twenty minutes or a half-hour passed before enemy mortar rounds were again falling along the ridgeline. Flares popped overhead, and the bugle calls and whistles resumed, along with shrieks of ``Kill! Kill! Kill!''

Miyamura hurled more grenades and emptied his carbine, watching advancing figures move up the slope toward his position.

Forgotten No More

Off to his right, the heavy machine gun continued firing, but there was silence from the .30-caliber light-machine-gun position on his left. Clambering out of his hole, he crawled to his left flank. The light weapon and its crew nowhere to be found and he wondered if they had "bugged out"?

Rejecting the idea, Miyamura reasoned that a runner must have instructed them to withdraw. But why hadn't the runner notified him? The answer came when, scrambling back toward the heavy-machine-gun position, he stumbled over a body and fell flat on his face. As a flare popped overhead, he saw that the body was one of H Company's runners, explaining why he hadn't gotten the message to withdraw.

Miyamura returned to the heavy machine-gun position to find two of the four GIs in the machine-gun position wounded by shrapnel, and he dressed their wounds. Instructing them to cover him, he clamped his bayonet on his carbine and left the emplacement, sliding down the slope toward the enemy. Minutes later, there were agonizing cries in the darkness from the direction he had gone.

Using his bayonet, Miyamura killed approximately ten of the enemy in close hand-to-hand combat. Chinese soldiers had been moving up the slope when Miyamura suddenly appeared, Jabbing and slashing with his bayonet, scattering one group, then shifting to attack another group in the same way.

Miyamura moved back up the slope to the machine-gun position and ordered the gunners and the two wounded riflemen to fall back while he remained behind to cover them.

Suddenly alone and frightened, he awaited the next attack. Shortly after, bugles and whistles sounded, and the chants of the enemy grew louder and closer as Miyamura opened fire, continuing until he ran out of ammunition, then he began tossing grenades in the enemy's direction.

Determining that it was time to withdraw, he first he had to destroy the heavy machine gun and he placed a grenade, its pin already pulled in the gun's open breach, then he ran to a nearby trench.

Moving down the trench, Miyamura collided with an enemy soldier and he shot the Chinese soldier wounding him, but not before the Chinese soldier threw a grenade in Miyamura's direction. It was beginning to grow light in the east as the enemy swarmed over the ridge he had evacuated.

He spotted a friendly tank that had been staked out to cover the withdrawal and he saw that it was getting ready to pull back. Miyamura, in pain from his wounds made a desperate dash toward it, but he stumbled and fell into barbed wire as, writhing in pain, he heard the tank rumble off.

Miyamura painfully managed to untangle himself from the wire and crawled into a small shell hole, hurting from the barbed-wire punctures and from the grenade-fragment wounds in his leg.

Enemy troops swarmed down the slope and passed by the hole where he lay, paying little attention to what they must have thought was a dead GI. Hoping that he could make it through the day by playing dead, he might be able to make it back to his own lines when night fell. It was not to be. A lone enemy soldier stopped beside him and pressing a U.S. Army 45-caliber pistol at his head said in English ``Get up, I know you're alive. We

don't harm prisoners.''

Four days later, when a 3rd Division task force fought its way back to the position Miyamura had evacuated, Miyamura was not among the dead GIs who lay there with more than 50 enemy dead, scattered around his position.

As his Medal of Honor citation would later state; "*When last seen, he was fighting ferociously against an overwhelming number of enemy soldiers*" and Miyamura was listed as Missing in Action". It would be many months before the U. S. government would be notified that he was a prisoner of war.

For Miyamura, his ordeal was far from over. Joining other POWs, he was marched north, assisting another wounded POW, Joe

Forgotten No More

Annello, until being threatened if he didn't put Annello down. Prisoners unable to keep up were frequently shot, and threatened with being shot, Annello persuaded Miyamura to set him down and the two were separated.

They were marched 300 miles over the next five weeks, with no food the first two weeks, no medical attention to the wounded and the only water was from streams. *"There were times I felt like giving up"* Miyamura recalled, *"The main thing that kept me going was faith in God and country."*

They finally arrived at Camp 1 at Changsong, near the Yalu River and about 20 miles from the North Korea/China border. Known as "Death Valley" by the POWs, the camp was rife with dysentery and malnutrition. Housed in huts with mud walls and dirt floors, and crowded by 9-12 POWs per hut, it was still an improvement over sleeping in the open

Fed a starvation diet of soybean milk, sorghum, millet and occasionally rice, the prisoners soon weakened making them more susceptible to disease and indoctrination, and the brutality of the guards. Being Asian earned Miyamura special attentions from his captors.

Miyamura endured almost 28 months of captivity, from April 25, 1951 until August 20, 1953, when he and nineteen other POW's boarded trucks headed for Panmunjon.

One of the first thing Miyamura did upon his release was to send a telegram to his wife Terry. It read; *"My Dearest Terry, Never so happy to be American as today. Your prayers for me have been answered. Am feeling OK. Getting wonderful care. Don't worry about me. On my way home by boat. Longing to see you again. Best Wishes to all- Hirsh"*

Miyamura arrived in San Francisco on September 5, 1953 aboard the troop ship USNS *Marine Addler* (T-AP-193) and he was given the honor of being the first man down the gangplank. He went home on leave to Gallup, where businesses and schools were closed in his honor.

Hiroshi Miyamura

Miyamura received an honorable discharge from the Army on October 10, 1953 and was promoted to Staff Sergeant and awarded the Medal of Honor by President Eisenhower in a White House ceremony on October 27, 1953, only the second Japanese American to be awarded the medal. The first, PFC Sadeo Munimori, was awarded posthumously at the end of WW II in April, 1945.

Miyamura's Medal of Honor had been awarded on December 21, 1951 but had been classified "Top Secret" out of fear that Miyamura's captors would seek retribution or abuse him because of his actions.

Miyamura returned to Gallup, to open a filling station and parts store where he worked as a mechanic and raised his family. Almost a year after his return from the war, Miyamura was surprised when a man who he thought was dead walked into his store. It was Joe Annello. Rather than being killed, he managed to escape a few weeks after he and Hershey were separated. Both men had believed the other was dead.

"Hershey" continues to live in Gallup today, aged 95. He frequently speaks at patriotic or veteran events, sharing the message *"There's always a greater plan. Keep the faith. Never give up."*

Forgotten No More

Sources;

Bartelt, Eric S. *Secret Hero Recounts his Unforgettable Korean War* American Forces Press Service, April 24, 2001

Congressional Record: March 22, 2001 (Senate) Page S2725-S2726

Hymoff, Edward. *For More Than Two Years, Hiroshi Miyamura's Medal of Honor Was a Tightly Guarded Secret* Military - History Magazine April, 1996

Lange, Katie. *Korean War POW Earns Medal of Honor for Saving His Unit* Dept. of Defense News, may 14, 2017

Mozingo, Joe. *Hiroshi Miyamura and his Hometown had a lot in common. They Believed in America* Los Angeles Times, July 3, 2017

US National Archives and Records Administration (NARA) WWII Enlistment Record # 39868194 (Miyamura, Hiroshi)

Walz, Kent. *Face-to-Face with Hiroshi Miyamura: Journey from 'enemy alien' to American hero* Albuquerque Journal (NM) March 3, 2018

CHAPTER TWELVE

HAROLD GUSTAV "SWEDE" CARLSON
Last use of aerial torpedoes

On April 22, 1951 the Chinese Communists (PVA) launched a Spring Offensive, also known as the Chinese Fifth Phase Offensive, sending three field armies, approximately 700,000 south to permanently drive United Nations forces from the Korean peninsula. It was the largest Communist offensive since Nov.-Dec. 1950. Colliding with US I Corps and IX Corps, the advance was halted north of Seoul by April 30.

Rear Admiral Ralph A. Oftstie, commander of Task Force 77 in the Sea of Japan, aware of the Chinese forces massive spring offensive, realized that something had to be done to stop the Chinese advance and to him the quickest, most sure way to slow the onslaught was to eliminate the Hwachon Dam, the great hydroelectric plant on the Pukhan River. By destroying the floodgates, the level of the river would rise creating a natural barrier to the enemy's advance

The problem was that the Hwachon Dam was 240 feet thick at its base fortified by rocks on both ends. The structure so massive that an earlier raid by B-29 bombers had failed to knock it out of commission. So now commanders at US Eighth Army looked to the Navy for a solution.

Admiral Oftslie assigned the mission to Captain William O. Gallery, commanding the aircraft carrier USS *Princeton* (CV-37) and the Commander-Air Group (CAG) of Carrier Air Group 19 (CVG-19), Commander Richard C. Merrick.

Forgotten No More

Ultimately, the responsibility for taking out the Hwonchon Dam would fall to Medium Attack Squadron 195 (VA-195) and its skipper, Lt. Cmdr. Harold "Swede" Carlson.

Harold Gustav "Swede" Carlson was born in Portland, Oregon on February 2, 1917 the older of two sons born to Sven and Inanna Carson, Swedish immigrants who instilled in them a sense of honesty, tenacity, kindness and humor, even as they later faced the challenges of the Great Depression. A brilliant student, Carlson was appointed to the U.S. Naval Academy in 1936.

Lt. Cmdr. Harold "Swede" Carlson

Upon his graduation from Annapolis on June 6, 1940, Carlson was commissioned an ensign and was assigned aboard the Brooklyn-class cruiser USS *Nashville* (CL-43), as the Gunnery and Engineering Officer. The *Nashville* escorted the USS *Hornet* (CV-8) on the Doolittle Tokyo Raid on April 18, 1942, shortly after the United States entry into WW II.

Carlson was accepted for flight training in September 1942 and he trained at New Orleans, Louisiana and Pensacola and Fort Lauderdale, Florida, being designated a naval aviator on April 9, 1943.

In November 1943, Carlson was ordered to report to San Diego, California as executive officer (XO) of Torpedo Squadron 20 (VT-20) flying Grumman TBM-3 *Avenger* torpedo-bombers. In February 1944, Carlson was transferred to Composite Squadron 11 (VC-11), a pioneer in AEW (Airborne Early Warning) warfare.

The squadron embarked aboard the newly commissioned USS *Nehenta Bay* (CVE-74) a Casablanca-class escort carrier.

Harold "Swede" Carlson

Following its shakedown cruise, and transport runs to Pearl Harbor, Hawaii and back, the *Nehenta Bay* departed Pearl Harbor on June 18, bound for combat in the Mariana.

The carrier operated off the newly captured Eniwetok Atoll and Carlson flew anti-submarine patrols and close air support missions during the Battle of Tinian, attacking enemy gun emplacements on July 5 and 7.

Following refueling and replenishment, the *Nehenta Bay* conducted anti-submarine operations off Guam and Saipan and launching strike on Saipan. At the end of the *Nehenta Bay's patrol*, Carlson transferred to the USS *Rocky Mount* (AGC-3) an Appalachian-class command ship in September where he flew combat missions in support of the landing at Leyte in the Philippines.

In November 1944, Carlson returned stateside and was undergoing additional flight training when the war ended in September 1945. He finished the war with the award of an Air Medal and a Purple Heart.

In June 1950, Carlson, now a lieutenant commander took over as skipper of Attack Squadron 195 (VA-195) *"Satan's Kitten"* and departed NAS Alameda for Korea aboard the newly-recommissioned USS *Princeton* (CV-37)

Upon their arrival in Korea in December of 1950, Carlson led VA-195 in ground support missions, including supporting the Marines in their evacuation and fighting withdrawal from the Chosin Reservoir back to Hungnam.

VA-195's close support undoubtedly saved U.S. lives in the evacuation. On one mission, Carlson made a virtual dead stick landing on the USS *Boxer* in Wonsan Harbor after his plane was hit by enemy fire.

In March of 1951, Carlson led his squadron in destroying a 600-foot railway bridge-tunnel complex south of Kilchu, North Korea. This took a sustained effort and numerous strikes as the Communists rebuilt the bridge each night.

Forgotten No More

Admiral Ofstie, TF-77 commander, was so pleased with the effort that he named the target area Carlson's Canyon. James Michener's book *"The Bridges at Toko-Ri"* is based in part on Carlson's Canyon.

Now, in late April, Carlson and VA-195 were presented with the challenge of taking out the Hwachon Dam.

On April 30, the CAG, Cmdr. Merrick led Carlson and five other Douglas A-1 *Skyraider* fighters of VF-195 and five F4U-4 *Corsairs* of VF-193, under the command of Lt. Cmdr. E.A. Parker on a raid on the dam. The *Skyraiders* would attack the gates with 2000 lb. bombs and 11.75 "Tiny Tim" rockets. The *Corsairs*, armed with 100 and 500 lb. bombs, would provide flak suppression.

Merrick himself was a colorful character, a WW II veteran who always flew with 7X50 binoculars, a K-20 aerial camera, and a German luger pistol who had assumed command of CVG-19 on July 7, 1950.

The dam was a difficult target as 4,000-foot ridges surrounded the reservoir limiting access to only two aircraft at a time, making their runs against such a tiny target extremely difficult. Added to that was the threat from enemy anti-aircraft batteries.

As the first pair flew into the valley, Communist batteries opened up with heavy ground fire. Swooping in low, the *Corsairs* targeted every anti-aircraft site they could identify, searching frantically for the telltale puffs that marked the guns, while the *Skyraiders* flew the gauntlet in rapid succession, straddling the dam and inflicting minor damage but none of the bombs hit the vital gates, while the rockets simply skittered off the dam, doing no damage.

The mission was a success only in the fact that no aircraft were lost, but there was no significant damage to the dam. At the mission debriefing, Capt. Gallery suggested the use of MK-13 anti-ship torpedoes. There were several drawbacks to the plan.

For one thing, although prior to sailing they had taken aboard nearly a dozen MK 13 torpedoes, leftovers from WW II, while at the

Puget Sound Navy Yard at Bremerton, Washington, no one was exactly sure of just where the MK 13 torpedoes were stored.

Another problem was that the carrier's ordnance men had absolutely no idea how to hang torpedoes from the *Skyraider*'s belly and had to consult a dogeared technical manual for help. Undeterred, the crew eventually located the torpedoes and worked through the night to mount them properly.

Only three pilots aboard Princeton had ever dropped a "tin fish" before; and of the remaining pilots chosen to fly the mission, most, like Ensign Robert E. Bennett, had never even seen an aerial torpedo. Three aviators from VC-35 "Night Hecklers" who had some experience with torpedo drops, Lieutenants Arthur Clapp, Frank Metzner and Addison English, were selected to fly the mission.

There were also tactical considerations. As Bennett later explained "If released *too high, the torpedo would enter the water steeply and dive. Too low and the torpedo would skip off the water. There was difficulty also in slowing down to maximum drop speed, and if the ball wasn't centered, the torpedo wouldn't run true. The torpedoes were finicky little devils.*"

Forgotten No More

Early on May 1, Merrick led his second strike, consisting of eight *Skyraiders* from VA-195 and three from VC-35, each carrying a single torpedo, backed up by eight *Corsairs* from VF-192 and four from VF-193. Looking ungainly with their torpedoes slung under their bellies, the *Skyraiders* had been designed with just such a mission in mind. The attack required them to fly in low, drop their torpedo, then climb sharply to avoid the dam itself.

Carlson led the attack, diving in and taking hits from Soviet M1939 37mm cannon fire, one round punching a hole so close to his legs it tore his flight suit. Fearlessly ignoring the flak, he lined up his shot and dropped his torpedo, pulling up and right as another shower of glowing enemy fire drilled through his starboard wing.

The torpedo impacted on target near a floodgate. Six more *Skyraiders* took their shots, each under intense enemy fire from angry gunners positioned around the dam. Six of the eight Mark 13s struck on or near the floodgates, with the center sluice floodgate blown to bits and an interior gate damaged. The dam was breached and holed on both sides. But their success was not without cost.

The eighth and final *Skyraider*, piloted by Lt. Jason Pressure, leveled his wings and bore in, defiant of the danger. Being the last in, the North Koreas were ready and unleashed fire so fierce it was a miracle that Pressure wasn't immediately blown out of the sky as he started his run.

Sadly, his torpedo was released too soon and too low, and it skipped over the dam's rim. As he pulled up to starboard, a fusillade of 37-mm. shells struck the front of the aircraft, the engine exploding like a bomb, Pressure having no chance to eject as his *Skyraider* buckled and crashed and burst into fire.

Still, the mission's results were remarkable. The heavy damage destroyed electrical power over a vast area, and the dam's destruction and the subsequent flooding seriously hindered the enemy's offensive. In every way, the damage inflicted by the torpedoes exceeded every expectation. From that point forward, VA-195 would be forever known as "The Dam Busters".

Harold "Swede" Carlson

For the next three months, *Princeton's* air assets flew missions destroying highway and railroad bridges, hydroelectric plants and enemy gun positions as well as providing close air support to ground forces. In August, at the end of her deployment, the Princeton departed Korea for the U.S. arriving in San Diego on August 29.

For Carlson, it would be his last combat. In October, he was assigned to a staff position in Washington DC and he would finish the war with the award of a Distinguished Flying Cross and three additional Air Medals.

For his part in leading the mission, Richard Merrick would be awarded the Navy Cross, but the award would be posthumous as Merrick would be killed in action while flying in support of the Marines on May 18, 1951, ten days short of his 40th birthday.

Carlson retired from active duty with the rank of full commander on July 1, 1961 with 21 years of service. He settled his family in the Bay Area where he had a 20 plus career as an Aeronautical Engineer.

On March 13, 2017, "Swede" Carlson took his final flight, passing away at the ripe age of 100 years, 1 month, 11 days. When asked what his greatest achievement was, Carlson would often answer that he was most proud that as commanding officer of VA-195, he only lost one pilot.

SOURCES:

Bloodsworth, C. Ross, and Evans, Mark L. *The Dam Busters at Hwachon* Naval Aviation News, March-April 2001

Burgess, Rick and Thompson, Warren. *AD Skyraider Units of the Korean War* Bloomsbury Publishing, (2016)

The Golden Eagles - *Harold G. Carlson, Commander, USN* http://www.epnaao.com/BIOS_files/EMERITUS/Carlson-%20Harold%20G.pdf

Hallion, Richard. *The Naval Air War in Korea*, Zebra Books, 1988.

Forgotten No More

Manson, Frank A. and Cagle, Malcolm W. *The Sea War in Korea*, Naval
    Institute Press , Annapolis (1957)

Harold "Swede" Carlson

CHAPTER THIRTEEN

JOHN KELVIN KOELSCH
First Pilot awarded the Medal of Honor

The Korean War saw some of the first practical operational uses of the helicopter in an active battle zone. Although developed toward the end of WW II, helicopters would be utilized for the first time in roles as diverse as transporting troop and supplies, reconnaissance and battlefield command and control.

And, the helicopter's role in evacuating the wounded to MASH units and offshore hospital ships cannot be overstated. Dubbed "Angels of Mercy" by the troops, one Army historian would later declare *""Few technical innovations were equal in importance to the growing use of the helicopter for medical evacuations,"*

The Sikorsky HO3S-1 *Dragonfly*, a light utility helicopter, was the Navy version of Sikorsky's commercial S-51 and was the first Navy helicopter to replace fixed wing aircraft operating with the fleet. From the 1920s on, seaplanes were the aircraft carried aboard battleships and cruisers. Now in Korean War, helicopters would continue the role of retrieving downed aircrews, not infrequently from behind enemy lines.

On July 3, 1951, a *Dragonfly* (Bu No. 1122175) of Helicopter Squadron #2 (HU-2) lifted off from its base aboard USS LST-488 (Landing Ship Tank), converted into a helicopter support ship designated Q-009, and stationed off the coast of North Korea on a mission to rescue a downed Marine aviator 35 miles southwest of Wonson in the Anbyon Valley, trapped behind enemy lines.

Both the pilot, Lieutenant (J.G.) John Koelsch, and his crewman, Aviation Machinist Mate 3rd Class (AM3C), George M.

Forgotten No More

Neal had volunteered for the extremely hazardous mission of rescuing the downed airman from behind enemy lines, and their actions would lead to the award of a Navy Cross and a Posthumous Medal of Honor.

John Kelvin Koelsch was in the family home at 2 Draycott Place, Chelsea, a borough London, England on December 22, 1923, the third son of Americans Henry August Koelsch, a banker and Beulah Anne Hubbard Koelsch. The family returned to America aboard White Star liner R.M.S. *Adriatic,* and departed Liverpool on April 26, 1934, and arrived at the Port of New York on May 5.

Koelsh attended boarding schools and two years at Princeton University in New Jersey before being accepted into the Naval Reserve on September 14, 1942 as an Aviation Cadet.

Graduating flight training on October 24, 1944, Koelsch was designated as a Naval Aviator and commissioned an ensign in the U.S. Navy. He was assigned to flying the Grumman TBM-3E *Avenger* torpedo-bomber assigned to Torpedo Squadron 97 (VT-97), where he served until the end of WW II.

Opting to remain in the Navy, he was promoted to lieutenant (junior grade) on August 1, 1946 and was assigned to Torpedo Squadron 18 (VT-18) in November 1946, re-designated as Attack Squadron 8A (VA-8A) on July 27, 1948.

While assigned to VA-8A, Koelsch embarked on two cruises aboard the newly commissioned USS *Leyte Gulf* (CV-32) an Essex-class aircraft carrier. This was followed by shore assignments at Princeton and Naval Air Station (NAS) Quonset Point, Rhode Island.

John Kelvin Koelsch

In 1948, Koelsch was assigned to Helicopter Development Squadron 3 (VX-3) at NAS Lakehurst (NJ) where he transitioned to rotary-powered aircraft (helicopters) flying the Sikorsky HO3S-1 *Dragonfly* and upon graduation on December 9, 1949, he was designated as a helicopter pilot. In August 1950, Koelsch was assigned to NAS Miramar

SIKORSKY HO#S-1 DRAGONFLY

Recognizing the value of helicopters in quickly rescuing downed pilots from the water, it became standard practice to assign a helicopter aboard every aircraft carrier and in October 1950, shortly after the start of the Korean War, Koelsch was assigned as Officer-in Charge (OIC) of the helicopter detachment aboard the USS *Princeton* (CV-37).

The *Princeton* departed San Diego, arriving off the Korean coast on December 5 to join Task Force 77 (TF-77) flying combat support missions as U.S. and U.N. forces began their withdrawal from the Chosin Reservoir. While aboard, Koelsch earned a reputation as a guy *"always ready for a rescue, no matter how dangerous"* making two rescues, as well as helping develop innovations like the floating rescue sling for operations over the water.

When the *Princeton* finished its deployment in May 1951, Koelsch requested and was granted permission to remain in Korea. In June, was transferred as OIC for HU-2 at Wonson, after telling his superiors that he wanted to remain until the job was done.

On July 3, 1951, Captain James V. Wilkins, a Marine *Corsair* pilot with Marine Fighter Squadron 312 (VMF-312) aboard the aircraft carrier USS *Sicily* (CVE-118), was flying a combat mission near Wonsan, North Korea, when his aircraft was struck by Chinese anti-aircraft fire, setting his plane on fire and causing him to quickly lose altitude.

Wilkins radioed for help and severely burned and with an injured left leg, he climbed out of the cockpit, and jumped. While parachuting to the ground, he saw his *Corsair* slam into the side of a nearby mountain and explode.

Wilkins landed in the Anbyon Valley, about 35 miles southeast of Wonson, in enemy held territory. Coming under fire from Chinese infantry, Wilkins crawled up the side of the mountain.

Koelsch and Neal volunteered for the rescue mission despite warnings that rescuing Wilkins would be near impossible due to the heavy ground resistance expected, Wilkins being deep in enemy territory, and the rapidly approaching night and thick fog making it unlikely he'd spot Wilkins even if flying right over him.

Taking off shortly before sunset, in a mist and low clouds and with darkness rapidly approaching, the slow moving, unarmed helicopter flew without a fighter escort due to the heavy fog that day, making such an escort impractical. Even without enemy fire, the combination of fog, approaching darkness, and the mountainous terrain made flying extremely hazardous.

Nonetheless, they took off, flying low below the cloud cover, sometimes just above tree-level, searching for the downed pilot.

Wilkins heard Koelsch's helicopter coming closer and moved down the mountain back towards where his parachute was. He saw the Sikorsky flying at about 50 feet below the clouds layer. The helicopter was receiving heavy ground fire from the Chinese soldiers along the road, sending bullets and shrapnel ripping through the aircraft. Koelsch, however, refused to abort the mission.

Taking several hits, Koelsch turned his aircraft away, but he quickly returned to locate Wilkins and hovered above him as Chinese troops sent bullets and shrapnel ripping through the aircraft. Koelsch, however, refused to abort the mission, taking intense fire while Neal lowered a "horse collar" harness on a hoist cable. Neal then lifted the fighter pilot up to the helicopter.

John Kelvin Koelsch

"It was the greatest display of guts I ever saw," Wilkins later recalled.

As Koelsch's Medal of Honor citation would document, *"Despite the increasingly intense enemy fire, which struck his helicopter on one occasion, he persisted in his mission until he succeeded in locating the downed pilot, who was suffering from serious burns on the arms and legs. While the victim was being hoisted into the aircraft, it was struck again by an accurate burst of hostile fire and crashed on the side of the mountain. Quickly extricating his crewmen and the aviator from the wreckage, Lt. (J.G.) Koelsch led them from the vicinity in an effort to escape from hostile troops, evading the enemy forces for nine days and rendering such medical attention as possible to his severely burned companion until all were captured"*

His engine damaged by enemy fire, Koelsch made a controlled crash into the mountainside and the aircraft rolled upside down. Koelsch and Neal emerged unhurt and Wilkins suffered no new injuries. Koelsch and Neal carried Wilkins and they evaded the enemy forces, heading toward the coast.

Traveling at night for seven days, they arrived at a coastal fishing village, weak and exhausted from no food for nine days. They found an abandoned house to hide in, but they were discovered with three hours. Captured, they were tied up and paraded before the villagers who subjected them to verbal and physical abuse. Taken to headquarters, the wounded Wilkins was separated from Koelsch and Neal, and was ultimately imprisoned at "Bean Camp", 45 miles southeast of Pyongyang.

While a prisoner, Koelsch shared his meager rations and angered his captors by constantly arguing for better conditions, earning him beatings and torture, but he *"steadfastly refused to aid his captors in any manner and served to inspire his fellow prisoners by his fortitude and consideration for others."*

Koelsch died of malnutrition and dysentery while a prisoner on October 16, 1951 and was awarded a posthumous Medal of Honor for his actions on July 3, 1951, and for his *"great personal valor and heroic spirit of self-sacrifice"* as a prisoner of war.

Forgotten No More

On August 3, 1955, his mother was presented his Medal of Honor in a ceremony at the Pentagon by Secretary of the Navy Charles S. Thomas, the first time a helicopter pilot was awarded the nation's highest medal for valor.

Following the Korean Armistice Agreement, Koelsch's remains were returned to the United States and interred in Section 30, Arlington National Cemetery, on October 14, 1955. On June 10, 1967, the USS *Koelsch* (FF-1049) a Garcia-class destroyer escort, later reclassified as a frigate, was commissioned and named in his honor.

Both Neal and Wilkens survived their captivity and were released on September 5, 1953. Neal was later awarded the Navy Cross for his actions on July 3, 1951. Neal passed away on December 1, 2016 at the age of 86 and is buried in Arlington National Cemetery. An Arleigh Burke-class guided-missile destroyer, USS *George M. Neal* DDG 131 named in his honor is planned to be commissioned in the near future.

John Kelvin Koelsch

Upon arriving in Korea, Koelsch wrote out his last will and testimony, in which he included his belief that "*A man who has failed to merit the attention of posterity in life cannot obtain it by means of a monument and plaque after death.*" His Medal of Honor is testimony that he merits the attention of posterity.

SOURCES:

John Kelvin Koelsch Biography - Naval History and Heritage Command - https://www.history.navy.mil/our-collections/photography/us-people/k/koelsch-john-kelvin.html

Naval Aviation News - Volumes 81-82 https://www.google.com/books/edition/Naval_Aviation_News/BnWoJha6LaMC?hl=en&gbpv=1&dq=john+kelvin+koelsch&pg=RA5-PA24&printsec=frontcover

Smallwood, Karl. *The Badass Story of the First Helicopter Pilot to Receive the Medal of Honor* http://www.todayifoundout.com/index.php/2018/11/the-badass-story-of-the-first-helicopter-pilot-to-receive-the-medal-of-honor/

Swopes, Bryan R. *This Day in Aviation website - July 3, 1951* https://www.thisdayinaviation.com/tag/james-v-wilkins/

Forgotten No More

CHAPTER FOURTEEN

DUANE E. DEWEY
A Body of Steel

145 Medals of Honor were awarded for actions during the Korean War, 103 of them Posthumously. Four were awarded to members of the Air Force, seven to the Navy, forty-two to Marines and ninety-two to the Army. 37 Medals went to officers, including a general, the remaining 108 to enlisted men. One went to a Chaplain. But all involved valor "above and beyond the call of duty."

It has become almost a cliché of valor, a soldier jumping on a hand grenade and selflessly covering it with his body to save his comrades with the subsequent award of the Medal of Honor, almost always awarded posthumously. And yet, despite almost certain death, there are numerous instances where men did exactly that. In United States military history, more citations for the Medal of Honor have been awarded for falling on grenades to save comrades than any other single act.

Pfc Sadeo Munimori, the first Japanese-American to be awarded the Medal of Honor, jumped on a grenade in Italy during WW II. As did Cpl. Williams Perkins Jr., a combat-photographer, during Vietnam. As did Jason Dunham in Iraq and Michael Monsoor, a Navy SEAL. All received posthumous Medals of Honor.

But not all awards are posthumous. Capt. Riley Pitts smothered a grenade during Vietnam, but it failed to explode. He survived only to be killed in battle days later. Jacklyn Lucas, at 17 the youngest to be awarded the Medal of Honor smothered two grenades during WW II and survived, one failing to explode. More recently, Marine Cpl. Kyle Carpenter survived jumping on a grenade in

Forgotten No More

Helmund Province Afghanistan in 2010 and lived to accept the award.

Of the 145 Medals of Honor awarded in Korea, 23 of those were awarded for jumping on a grenade. Of those, 19 were awarded posthumously. Cpl. Duane E. Dewey was one of four to survive.

Duane Edgar Dewey was born Grand Rapids, Michigan on November 16, 1941. His family moved to Muskegon in 1942, during WW II, and lived in temporary apartments built for factory workers. He attended Muskegon High School until the age of 16. *"The principal asked me to quit,"* he said. *"I was skipping school too much."*

He later went to live with aunt and uncle outside of South Haven and worked on a farm and then at a foundry, before enlisting in the Marine Corps Reserves on March 7, 1951 at age 19.

The War in Korea was underway, and his enlistment was indefinite, for the duration of the war and six months. After recruit training at Parris Island, SC and advanced combat training at Camp Pendleton, California, Dewey returned home on leave prior to shipping out for Korea and he married Bertha Bierhalter on May 14, 1951.

He departed for Korea in July 1951, assigned to Second Battalion, Fifth Marines, part of the 1st Marine Division, which embarked at San Diego and sailed to Pusan, Korea. Dewey arrived in Korea as a corporal in charge of a machinegun squad, part of Company E, 2nd Battalion, 5th Marines. The 2/5th Marines is the most highly decorated battalion in Marine Corps history.

In August, the Battalion helped defend the Pusan Perimeter as part of the 1st Marine Provisional Brigade, the legendary "Fire

Duane E. Dewey

Brigade" against invading North Korean forces. The 2/5th also took part in the landing at Inchon, the liberation of Seoul and the Chosin Reservoir Campaign, and saw its share of combat.

On April 16, 1952, the battalion was dug in near Panmunjom in a series of outposts out beyond the main American force. Cpl. Dewey was in a reinforced platoon of about 80 men at one of these positions atop a hill when it was attacked by a battalion-size force of about 500 Chinese soldiers at around midnight.

His position was quickly overwhelmed and, carrying their machine guns with them, Dewey and his men continued firing as they fell back. Out of their foxholes and fighting on exposed ground, they tried to stabilize their position. *"We'd had so many casualties we'd had to pull back to a smaller perimeter,"* Dewey later recalled.

Dewey fired his gun in such sustained fire that he feared the barrel might melt as dead Chinese soldiers piled up on top of one another in front of his position.

Seeing that there were only three cans of ammunition left, he ran to another machine gun for more. As he returned, a grenade exploded at his feet knocking him down. Bleeding heavily from the thigh and groin, he lay on the ground, trying to get his bearing.

A Navy corpsman appeared, and as he knelt over Dewey and his assistant gunner to treat their wounds, another grenade hit the ground beside them. Dewey called out "grenade" and grabbed it.

He considered throwing it back but decided he didn't have the time or the strength.

"I really didn't know where all my men were. I knew where my gunner and assistant gunner were, but I didn't know where my six ammo carriers were. I didn't want to heave (the grenade) out there in the dark and hit one of my ammo carriers. If you throw it out there and hear one of your own men scream and know it was you who threw it," he said later in an interview, *"You'd live with that the rest of your life."* Tucking the grenade underneath him, Dewey pulled the corpsman down with his other hand and yelled, "Hit the dirt, Doc."

Forgotten No More

The grenade detonated, lifting Dewey off the ground and tearing up his hip and groin with more shrapnel. The corpsman was uninjured. Dewey was taken back to the field aid station. For an hour he lay outside waiting for treatment, not sure that he would make it.

Dewey was given a shot of morphine and taken to a small underground bunker with other Marine casualties. He spent the rest of the night wondering which side would win the battle that was still raging outside and praying for his wife and the young child he had never seen.

Shortly after dawn, when American troops relieved his company, he was evacuated to a MASH. Doctors treating him in the field hospital found that in addition to the gaping shrapnel wounds throughout the lower part of his body, he had also taken a bullet in the stomach.

He was flown to Japan and hospitalized at the US Naval Hospital in Yokosuka for a month, then flown to the States, where he would spend

three more months convalescing first at the Naval Hospital at Mare Island, California, then at Great Lakes, Illinois.

Retired from active duty, he was honorably discharged on August 19, 1952 and returned home to Michigan to meet his infant daughter.

While on a stopover in Hawaii, Dewey had been presented with a Purple Heart Medal, and he'd heard that he might be nominated for the Medal of Honor. Dewey was home in South Haven, Michigan, when he was informed by telegram that he had been awarded the Medal of Honor.

On Wednesday, March 11, Dewey, his wife, Bertha; his parents, Mr. and Mrs. Ernest E. Dewey and his sister, Clara Jean Dewey traveled to Washington DC, where Dewey was fitted for a new uniform for the ceremony. The family found time to visit the Capitol, where they were greeted by Senator Charles E. Potter and Rep. Clare E. Hoffman of Michigan, who had been invited to accompany them to the White House.

Duane E. Dewey

12, 1953, Dewey participated in a Treasury Department bond sales program and then helped to complete the Department of Defense records on his citation prior to going to the White House.

On the morning of March 12, 1953, Dewey participated in a Treasury Department bond sales program and then helped to complete the Department of Defense records on his citation prior to going to the White House.

In an early afternoon ceremony in the Oval Office, with his family present, President Dwight Eisenhower presented Dewey with the Medal of Honor.

It was Eisenhower's first time conferring the Medal and as he draped the award around Dewey's neck, Eisenhower mused "*You must have a body of steel.*" After reviewing his citation, the President joked, telling the young medal winner that the grenade he smothered must have been an enemy grenade because "*if it had been one of ours, it would have blown you to pieces.*"

Forgotten No More

Later that day, Dewey traveled to New York City to appear on national television. He returned to Washington the next day to rejoin his family and have a few hours of sightseeing before his return trip home to western Michigan.

Dewey and his wife returned home after a week in Washington to a great surprise: To honor him, the townspeople had built a three-bedroom home, fully furnished and with a full pantry in his honor.

Released from active duty, Dewey worked as a damper-fitter in the Everett Piano factory in South Haven. Like most genuine heroes, he is modest about his recognition, stating *"I was only doing what anyone would do in that situation."*

Duane E. Dewey

Footnote: The following individuals were awarded posthumous Medals of Honor during the Korean War for smothering a hand grenade with their bodies;

Cpl. David Champagne	USMC	May 28, 1952
Cpl. John Collier	US Army	Sept. 19, 1950
Cpl. Gordon Craig	US Army	Sept. 10, 1950
Cpl. Jerry Crump	US Army	Sept. 7, 1950
Cpl. Jack Davenport	USMC	Sept. 21, 1951
Pfc. Fernando Garcia	USMC	Sept. 5, 1952
Pfc. Charles George	US Army	Nov. 30, 1952
Pfc. Edward Gomez	USMC	Sept. 14, 1951
Sgt. William Jecelin	US Army	Sept. 19, 1950
Pvt. Billie Kanell	USMC	Sept. 7, 1951
Pfc. Herbert Littleton	USMC	April 22, 1951
1Lt. Baldonero Lopez	USMC	Sept. 15, 1950
Pfc. Whitt Moreland	USMC	May 29, 1951
SFC. Donald Moyer	US Army	May 20, 1951
2Lt. Robert D. Reem	USMC	Nov. 6, 1950
SFC William Sitman	US Army	Feb. 14, 1951
2lt. Sherrod Skinner	USMC	Oct. 26, 1952
Pfc. David M. Smith	US Army	Sept. 1, 1950
Pfc. Henry Svehia	US Army	June 12, 1952
The following three individual survived to accept their awards;		
SSgt. Robert Kennemore	USMC	Nov. 28, 1950
Sgt. John Pittman	US Army	Nov. 26, 1950
Pfc. Robert Simanek	USMC	Aug. 17, 1952

Forgotten No More

Sources:

Duane E. Dewey Collection (AFC/2001/001/17946), Veterans History Project, American Folklife Center, Library of Congress

Gaertner, Eric. *Muskegon County's two Medal of Honor recipients being memorialized at Fruitport park*
https://www.mlive.com/news/muskegon/2011/05/muskegon_count ys_two_medal_of.html

List of Korean War Medal of Honor recipients
https://en.wikipedia.org/wiki/List_of_Korean_War_Medal_of_Hono r_recipients

Muskegon native who jumped on top of live grenade receives Congressional Medal of Honor from President Eisenhower
https://www.mlive.com/news/muskegon/2013/03/lookback_muske gon_native_who_j.html

CHAPTER FIFTEEN

DAVID BRUCE BLEAK
Combat Medic – Medal of Honor

The Korean War saw great advances in battlefield medicine which lowered the combat mortality rate from 4,5% in WW II to 2.5% during the conflict in Korea, with advances in medicines, surgical techniques and patient transportation, among others.

But it was the combat medic and corpsman, serving with the troops at the front, providing first aid and frontline trauma care, that was the vital first link that connected the wounded to the battalion aid station, MASH, Field Hospital, Evacuation Hospital and eventually Japan depending on the severity of the wound. The mission of the combat medic was to provide immediate medical care to wounded soldiers, not engage the enemy. And they were provided protection under the Geneva Convention

Chapter IV, Article 25 of the Geneva Convention states that: "*Members of the armed forces specially trained for employment, should the need arise, as hospital orderlies, nurses or auxiliary stretcher-bearers, in the search for or the collection, transport or treatment of the wounded and sick shall likewise be respected and protected if they are carrying out these duties at the time when they come into contact with the enemy or fall into his hands.*" It also states, "*Knowingly firing at a medic wearing clear insignia is a war crime.*"

Up until WWII, most medics were unarmed and wore distinctive red cross insignia on their helmets and brassards but Japan, not recognizing the Geneva Convention, specifically targeted medics and that practice quickly fell into disuse and this carried over into the Korean War.

As Carl Nussmeyer, a Korean War Medic, later reflected, "*I was with the men when they were fighting. I was actually a fighting soldier while taking care of somebody who's hurt. A medic has a helmet with a red cross on it,*

Forgotten No More

well that wasn't true at the time I was there. You carried a weapon of some kind, and you had a gunnysack over your helmet and to keep the noise down, you had your dog tags taped so they wouldn't jingle.

You would get a patrol order; and you went out in this valley between the two sides...When someone was wounded the only thing you could do was stop the bleeding and get him back to the aid station. That's the first stop. It was at least half a mile to a mile depending from the battle. Every circumstance is different. Somebody hollered in there, "Medic" you go out and get him, bring him in or work on him there."

Of the 146 Medals of Honor awarded during the Korean War, eight were awarded to medical personnel; 5 Navy corpsmen and 3 Army medics. Six (Edward Benfold USN, Richard De Wirt USN, Francis Hammond USN, John E. Kilmer USN, Richard G. Wilson USA and Bryant Womack USA) were awarded posthumously. Two, David Bleak USA and William Charette USN lived to receive the award.

Seven of the eight were awarded the medal for rendering aid under fire, two going so far as to shield the wounded with their own bodies. But only one medal would be awarded for hand-to-hand combat.

On June 14, 1952, a 20-man patrol from the 2nd Battalion of the 223rd Infantry Regiment's I&R (Intelligence and Reconnaissance) Platoon departed at dawn under cover of darkness to ascend the steep terrain of Hill 499. There were reports of Chinese troops operating in their area and their mission was to capture prisoners for interrogation.

Volunteering to accompany the patrol was Sgt. David Bleak, a medic attached to the unit's Medical Detachment. At 6'5 and 250 pounds, Bleak was described as quiet and easy-going, a "gentle giant" but his actions that day on Hill 499 were anything but gentle and would result in the award of the Medal of Honor.

David Bruce Bleak was born in Idaho Falls, Idaho on February 27, 1932, the seventh of nine children born to William and Tamar (Young) Bleak and he grew up during the Great Depression and WW II.

David Bruce Bleak

Bleak dropped out of high school and tried farming, ranching and working for a railroad before enlisting in the US Army on November 1, 1950 at the start of the Korean War.

After taking eight weeks of basic training at Fort Riley, Kansas, Bleak was selected for training as a medic and completed the basic combat medic course. He was assigned to the medical detachment of the 2nd Battalion, 223rd Infantry Regiment, 40th Infantry Division of the California Army National Guard.

At Camp Cooke in Lompoc, California, Bleak took advanced medical training and shortly after reporting in, the 40th Division, nicknamed "The Sunshine Division" was called up for deployment to Korea.

The division shipped out in March 1951 under the command of Major General Daniel Hudelson and spent the next nine months in Japan undergoing training in amphibious operations, air transport maneuvers and live fire exercises. On December 23, 1951, the division was put on alert for Korea and they arrived in Korea in early January 1952.

Forgotten No More

In February, after additional training, the division moved north to relieve the 24th Infantry Division at Minari-gol near the 38th parallel, now in North Korea.

By this period of the war, the front lines were for the most part stable and combat consisted of small, but constant skirmishes as both sides jockeyed for more territory, often the same hills, resulting in high casualty counts on both sides.

Now, on that crisp November morning, Bleak accompanied the I&R platoon as it slogged up the steep terrain. To the west, F Company of the 223rd engaged in a diversionary attack as the patrol moved higher.

Suddenly, Bleak heard heavy machinegun and automatic weapons fire and he rushed up from the rear of the patrol to find several of the lead element wounded. He treated and stabilized the wounded, then continued on with the patrol.

Nearing the summit, the patrol came under fire from Chinese soldier in a concealed trench, wounding another soldier. As stated in his Medal of Honor citation; *"Nearing the military crest of the hill, while attempting to cross the fire-swept area to attend the wounded, he came under hostile fire from a small group of the enemy concealed in a trench. Entering the trench, he closed with the enemy"*

As eyewitnesses later testified, an enraged Bleak "dove in" the trench and grabbing one Chinese soldier, snapped his neck with his bare hands and then grabbed a second soldier by his neck, crushing his windpipe. When a third soldier rushed him, he pulled his combat knife and thrust it into his chest, killing him.

Bleak returned to the patrol and was treating the wounded when an enemy grenade bounced off the helmet of a nearby soldier and rolled away. Tackling the dazed soldier, and with complete disregard for his own safety, he covered him with his large frame as the grenade exploded. Remarkably, the soldier was unhurt, and Bleak sustained only minor wounds.

The patrol continued on, successfully captured several Chinese soldiers, and began moving back down the hill toward UN lines when they again came under fire from another concealed trench, wounding another three soldiers. While treating their wounds, Bleak was himself wounded in the leg.

One of the three was too injured to walk, and despite his own wound and under enemy fire, Bleak lifted up the soldier and carried him down the hill. When Bleak was confronted by two Chinese soldiers wielding fixed bayonets, he put down the soldier and charging like a maddened bull he charged, grabbing the two and smashing their heads together with such force that he fractured their skulls.

All 20 members returned from the patrol, with one third wounded, and Bleak's actions were credited with saving the patrol by his treating the wounded and "neutralizing" five enemy soldiers.

Hospitalized for his wounds, Bleak was promoted to staff sergeant and returned to duty on July 9, 1952. When his tour of duty in Korea was complete, he finished his enlistment serving in Japan.

Shortly after his discharge, on October 27, 1953, Bleak along with six others (1Lt. Raymond G. Murphy, USMCR, 1Lt. James L. Stone, USA, 2Lt. George H. O'Brien, Jr., USMCR, Sgt. Hiroshi H. Miyamura, USA, Pfc. Alford L. McLaughlin, USMCR, and Pfc. Robert E. Simanek, USMCR) gathered on the North Portico of the

Forgotten No More

White House to be presented the Medal of Honor by President Dwight D. Eisenhower.

Struggling to clasp the award around Bleak's neck, Eisenhower whispered *"You have a damned big neck."*

Bleak returned to civilian life where he worked various jobs as a truck driver, a grocery store meat cutter, and a rancher in Idaho and later Wyoming. He married Lois Pickett in 1966 and had four children, moved to Moore, Idaho, and ran a dairy farm for 10 years. He eventually took a job as a janitor at the Idaho National Engineering Laboratory, where he worked his way up to chief hot cell technician, responsible for disposing of spent nuclear fuel rods. He retired in the mid-1990s.

Bleak died at the Lost Rivers District Hospital in Arco, Idaho, on 23 March 2006, from emphysema, Parkinson's disease, and complications from a hip fracture.

He died the same day as Desmond Doss, another medic and Medal of Honor recipient. His body was cremated, and his remains scattered at his favorite fishing location. His family later placed a memorial in his honor at the Lost River Cemetery in Butte County, Idaho.

As a postscript, another soldier, Corporal Clifton T. Speicher of F Company was awarded the Medal of Honor for his actions on June 14, most likely during the diversionary attack.

"On that day, during an attack against a hostile position near Minarigol, his squad came under intense small-arms, mortar, and machine gun fire. Although wounded, Speicher charged the machine gun nest and killed the occupants with his rifle and bayonet. He was wounded again during his approach and died shortly after silencing the emplacement. For these actions, he was posthumously awarded the Medal of Honor"

David Bruce Bleak

SOURCES:

Bernstein, Adam. *David Bleak, 74; Won Medal of Honor in Korea,* The Washington Post, March 31, 2006

Collier, Peter; Del Calzo, Nick. Medal of Honor: Portraits of Valor Beyond the Call of Duty, Workman Publishing NY (2006)

Freeman, Robert C.; Wright, Dennis A. *Saints at War: Korea and Vietnam.* Covenant Communications, UT (2003).

Greenwood, John T. Medics at war: Military medicine from colonial times to the 21st century, Naval Institute Press, MD (2006)

"Medal of Honor recipients". Korean War. United States Army Center of Military History. June 8, 2009. https://en.wikipedia.org/wiki/List_of_Korean_War_Medal_of_Hono r_recipients#Medal_of_Honor_recipients

Forgotten No More

CHAPTER SIXTEEN

ROYCE WILLIAMS
Top Secret Ace

On November 18, 1952, the aircraft carrier USS *Oriskany* (CV-34), the "Mighty O" was in the Sea of Japan offshore of Chonjin, North Korea in less than ideal conditions to launch a combat mission. A blizzard filled the grey skies and there was extremely low visibility with the cloud cover at 400 feet.

Part of the three-carrier Task Force 77, the Oriskany's Carrier Air Group 19 (CAG-19), had earlier in the day sent *Panther* fighters from VF-781 *"Pacemakers"* and VF-783 *"Minutemen"* as well as fighters from the other two carriers, had earlier in the day made a massive strike on the industrial complex at Hoeryong, near the North Korean/Russian border.

Anticipating a reprisal, Lt. Commander S.R. Holm, commanding officer of VF-781, was ordered to put up a Combat Air Patrol (CAP) to provide air cover for the task force.

Flight Leader, Lt. Claire Elwood and his wingman Lt. (jg) John Middletown and Section Leader, Lt. Royce Williams and his wingman Lt. (jg) David Rowlands were selected to fly CAP that day.

Soon after the CAP was launched, the Combat Information Center (CIC) reported multiple bogeys approaching inbound, 80 miles north of Task Force 77.

In a sequence of unforeseen circumstances, Lt. Williams would find himself alone facing six MiG-15 jet fighters. What would occur in the next 35 minutes would be classified Top Secret and remain unrevealed for 50 years.

Forgotten No More

Elmer Royce Williams was born in Wilmot, South Dakota on April 4, 1925, one of six children (2 boys, 4 girls) born to Elmer L. and Esther F. Williams. When he was 4 years old, a barnstormer landed in a nearby pasture and took him, his older brother Lynn and his 80-year-old grandmother up in a Ford Trimotor aircraft. From then on, both boys resolved to become aviators.

As a boy, he spent a lot of time fishing, playing hockey and, in his own words *"got in my share of trouble."* In 1936 his father, a WW I veteran used his veteran's bonus to buy a grocery store and he moved the family to the small rural town of Clinton Minnesota during the Great Depression.

It is said that he met his future wife, Camilla Forde, at the age of five, the first day of Sunday School, but they attended Clinton High School together, and he married her on June 1, 1947 at St. Paul Lutheran Church in Clinton.

While still in high school in 1941, at age 16, Williams enlisted in the Minnesota State Guard and graduated high school in 1943 having attained the rank of corporal. At the age of 17, he was accepted into the V-5 Aviation Cadet program reasoning that Annapolis and college, two other paths to a commission, were beyond his reach.

When the majority of his guard battalion was sent overseas to Morocco, Williams, too young to deploy, was sent to Camp Ripley, Minnesota for additional training. He also found time to quarterback the school's football team, earn the rank of Eagle Scout and graduate first in his class.

After graduation, Williams took a train with 250 others and reported to Corpus Christi, Texas on August 10, 1943 for Boot Camp. What followed was almost two years of flight training beginning with flight preparatory school at Murray, Kentucky and Conway, Arkansas for War Training School (WTS), flying the Naval Aircraft Factory N3N, a tandem-seat, open cockpit, the navy's primary training biplane aircraft, nicknamed "The Yellow Peril"

Following pre-flight training at the University of Georgia at Athens, Georgia in 1944. Williams took primary training at Memphis,

Tennessee, where he flew the N2S Boeing-Stearman Model 75 biplane, then finally to Pensacola, Florida where he flew the Vultee BT-13 trainer, then the T-6 *Texan*, an advanced trainer and finally the Douglas SBD *Dauntless*, a scout/dive bomber.

With demobilization following the end of WW II, Williams chose to remain in the Navy. On November 15, 1945, Williams achieved his childhood dream when he was commissioned an ensign in the naval reserve and designated a naval aviator. By early 1946, Williams was at Opa-Lacka, Florida, where he flew the Gruman F6F *Hellcat*. The *Hellcat* had a top speed of 375 MPH, a range of 1,089 miles and was armed with six machine guns. The aircraft was powered by an 18-cylinder Pratt and Whitney, air-cooled, radial engine.

Williams became carrier qualified (CARQUAL) aboard the USS *Ranger* (CV-4), the first U.S. vessel to be designed and built from the keel up as a carrier. After a brief period aboard the carrier USS *Franklin D. Roosevelt* (CV-42) "Rosie", Williams was ordered aboard the USS *Princeton* (CV-37) assigned to VBF-81 where he transitioned from the *Hellcat* to the Vought F4U *Corsair* and later the Gruman F8F *Bearcat,* all propeller-driven fighters.

From 1949, Williams attended University of Minnesota to earn a bachelor's degree, a requirement for a commission in the regular navy and was granted both a BA and regular commission in 1950, after finishing his course work at the US Naval Postgraduate School in Monterey, California.

"The Fight was on. They were no longer in formation. They were flying to position themselves to attack me one at a time," Williams later recalled *"There was a lot of maneuvering, some shooting and mostly dodging going on,"*

With the war going on in Korea, Williams, now a naval lieutenant, was assigned to fighter squadron VF-781 at Miramar NAS near San Diego where he transitioned to the Grumman F9F-5 *Panther*, the Navy's first carrier-based jet fighter, and took weapons training at El Centro, Ca.

The *Panther* had a maximum speed of 575 miles per hour at sea level, had a service ceiling of 44,600 feet and a range of 1,353

Forgotten No More

miles. The *Panther* was armed with four M3 20 mm autocannon placed in the nose with 760 rounds of ammunition. It could carry up to 3,000 pounds of bombs or eight 5-inch rockets on four hardpoints under each wing.

The F9F was widely used during the Korean War. Baseball legend Capt. Ted Williams flew 39 missions with the 223rd Fighter Squadron and Major John Glenn flew F9Fs with VF-311 flying a total of 90 missions, downing 3 MiGs and earning two Distinguished Flying Crosses (DFC). At one point, Williams was Glenn's wingman. Naval aviator Neil Armstrong, the first man on the moon, flew 78 combat missions from the deck of the USS *Essex* (CV-9)

The F9F was widely used during the Korean War. Baseball legend Capt. Ted Williams flew 39 missions with the 223rd Fighter Squadron and Major John Glenn flew F9Fs with VF-311 flying a total of 90 missions, downing 3 MiGs and earning two Distinguished Flying Crosses (DFC). At one point, Williams was Glenn's wingman. Naval aviator Neil Armstrong, the first man on the moon, flew 78 combat missions from the deck of the USS *Essex* (CV-9)

VF-781 embarked aboard the USS Oriskany shortly after arriving in San Diego on July 21, 1952. As part of Carrier Air Group 19 (CAG-19), the squadron conducted CARQUALs over the summer and the Oriskany departed for Korea on September 15, arriving at Yokosuka, Japan on October 19.

joining TF-77 on October 31, VF-781 flew the *Panther's* first combat mission, followed by others conducting bombing and strafing raids.

Now, on the afternoon of November 18, as the flight of four *Panthers* rose above the blizzard, they spotted seven contrails at 35,000 feet that were identified as Soviet MiG-15s.

Air combat during the Korean War was unique because most of the aerial combat was between Russian and American pilots rather than among the Koreans. The United Nations Command (UNC) flew some 700,000 sorties, with American pilots accounting for 93% of these sorties compared to the 90,000 sorties flown by Communist forces.

The lower number of Communist sorties likely resulted from Soviet Russia's (USSR) intention of limiting overt military assistance to the Democratic Peoples' Republic of Korea (DPRK) and the Peoples' Republic of China (PRC) / Chinese Communist Forces (CCF) in an effort to limit the conflict to the Korean peninsula.

Shortly after spotting the MiGs, the fuel pump warning light came on in Elwood's aircraft and he and his wingman Middleton were ordered to descend and provide air cover over the Oriskany, leaving Williams and Rowlands to provide a barrier between the MiGs and TF-77.

Williams recalled *"I felt my heart flutter. I suddenly realized that if things turned hot, the odds had just dropped from four against seven to only two against seven."*

Outnumbered 2-7, they were outclassed by the MiGs which had superior speed and a greater rate of climb. *"I knew that MiG-15s were faster and more maneuverable than our Panthers,"* Williams later remembered. *"I was really hoping we could scare them off because I didn't think we'd survive a head-to-head dogfight. Especially if they were being flown by experienced Soviet pilots."*

Williams and Rowlands ascended to 26,000 feet. When the Migs reversed course, Williams believed them headed back to their base at Vladivostok. But the seven MiGs then broke into two groups.

Forgotten No More

Four MiGs came straight at them from 10 O'clock while the other three circled and Williams turned into his attackers and when they overshot him, he made a hard left and got the trailing MiG in his sights and shot him down with his 20mm guns.

"The MiG's pilot jerked left and right to avoid my cannon fire, but not in time," Williams said. *"The guy fell out of formation trailing black smoke and a spray of airplane parts."*

Roland saw the lead MiG break away and followed him down to 8,000 feet to ensure he didn't crash into the carrier. Rowland tried to fire his guns at the MiG to finish him off, but his gun jammed. He finally broke off but was unable to rejoin Royce

Most of the pre-deployment combat training had focused on engaging targets on the ground with little air-to air combat training. What came next was incredible airmanship as Williams frantically attempted to evade his attackers and get them in his sights.

One of the three MiGs turned and came straight at him while the other two positioned themselves for a diving attack, and as Williams turned into the attack, they blasted him with cannon fire and he heard a dozen rounds strike the metal of his *Panther*.

Rowland had not yet returned, and Williams was all alone and facing three superior aircraft. They raced toward him with guns blazing and he wondered if his first dogfight would be his last.

As he rolled and banked, Williams thought he might survive the day until the three MiGs from the other sortie broke through the clouds to join their cohorts.

"One MiG managed to get behind me. I used a trick I'd been taught to make him overshoot my position. Then I did a loop and got on his six. I locked on and fired" Williams later stated.

The *Panther*'s rounds detonated against the MiG and the plane disintegrated. Parts exploded into the air, forcing Williams to evade the debris. He lined up on another MiG and fired. The Soviet plane broke away as the rounds appeared to hit but Royce didn't follow to verify. He was too busy trying to shake two more Soviets off his rear.

Royce Williams

Continuing evasive actions, Williams could hear rounds striking his fuselage as he went after another MiG and pounded it with 20 mm cannon fire. The MiG broke off in a trail of smoke. Then he heard several more rounds slam into the side of his plane. One of the MiGs 37-mm rounds had scored a hit in the right wing.

He felt the Panther shudder and discovered that he'd lost most of his rudder and aileron control. Only his elevators were still functioning normally, and his low fuel light came on. And he was out of ammunition.

At that point, outnumbered and in a damaged aircraft, Williams decided to give up the fight and head back toward the task force, but found that he was still being pursued. *"This guy just came around, and I can't turn,"* he recalled. *"He's maybe 400 feet behind me just firing away. But I would push over, and rounds would go over me. And I'd pull up, and they'd go under me until I got in the clouds, and I lost sight of him."*

Williams, knowing how slim his chances of survival would be, rejected ejecting out of the aircraft and instead opted for trying to land his plane on the *Oriskany*. Using gravity and pilot skill to lower the landing gear and tailhook, he headed toward the ship at nearly 200 mph.

As he neared the task force, the remaining MiGs retreated, but with his radio out of commission due to the damage he'd sustained, he had no way to communicate with the ship.

Worse, the task force had gone to general quarters with orders to open fire on any unidentified aircraft and since he couldn't communicate with them, they opened fire on Williams aircraft stopping only when he was close enough to identify.

Williams couldn't slow down, or he would stall which forced him to make his landing at 200 miles per hour. Incredibly, he was still able to catch the #3 wire on the flight deck and he emerged uninjured.

On the flight deck, the plane's 263 perforations were circled and counted, ranging from a foot wide to minor cuts in the fuselage. William's *Panther*, which had fought so gallantly was so badly damaged that they pushed it over the side into the ocean.,

Forgotten No More

Williams was called before the Captain and was ordered not to talk about his mission to anyone and advised him that it was classified as Top Secret. A fake report was sent to Washington, crediting Williams with a single kill and one probable damage, while Middleton was credited with a kill and Rowlands a probable.

Even though Williams "knew Rowlands never fired a shot," he was told to remain silent and ordered to meet with Vice Adm. Robert Briscoe, Commander, Naval Forces - Far East when the *Oriskany* reached Yokosuka, Japan, a week later.

Briscoe told Williams he would be credited with at least three kills but that he must never speak of the incident. It wasn't just the risk of dragging the Soviets into a broader conflict; the United States didn't want to reveal the existence of the brand-new National Security Agency (NSA).

Royce Williams

An NSA team aboard the heavy cruiser USS *Helena* (CA-75) had been testing new communications equipment that was intercepting radio chatter from the Soviets, and should the details of Williams' mission go public, the Soviets would know the United States could hear their communications, compromising the operation.

According to the NSA report, which wasn't declassified until July 15, 2015, it documented at least three kills by Williams, and following the end of the Cold War, Russian sources confirmed Williams' achievement, stating that the four pilots lost were Captains Belyakov and Vandalov, and Lieutenants Pakhomkin and Tarshinov.

A month later, Admiral J.J. Clark and Williams met with President-elect Eisenhower in Seoul, Korea. Eisenhower specifically requested a debriefing with Williams to discuss "our planes versus theirs." Also present were Generals Omar Bradley and Mark Clark, and Admiral Arthur Radford, the Secretary of Defense.

Williams continued flying combat missions, for a total of 70, and was awarded the Silver Star in April. The Oriskany departed Korea on April 22, 1953. In a career that would span over 32 years and include assignments as varied as a two-year assignment as an exchange pilot with the US Air Force at Nellis AFB flying the F-86 *Sabre* and the F-100 *Super Sabre*, the Armed Forces Staff College, Executive Officer (XO) and commanding officer (CO) of VF-33 aboard the nuclear USS *Enterprise* (CVA(N)-65, Captain of the USS *El Dorado* (LCC-11) and flying 110 combat missions in Vietnam from 1965-67.

Williams retired from the Navy on September 1, 1975 and his awards include the Silver Star, Legion of Merit with a combat "V", the Distinguished Flying Cross and the Bronze Star. Recently, efforts have been made to get his achievements recognized with the award of the Medal of Honor.

Williams' attack on those seven MiGs that November day prevented an attack on the entire task force and undoubtedly saved lives. When asked how he survived the dogfight unscathed, he modestly responds;

Forgotten No More

"I'm a God-fearing person. And I had done a whole lot more training than the other guys up there."

SOURCES:

Howard, Henry. *Silent Hero* American Legion Magazine, Sept. 23, 1968

Early and Pioneer Naval Aviators Association, Williams Bio
http://www.epnaao.com/BIOS_files/REGULARS/Williams-%20E%20Royce.pdf

Rooney, Austin. *Top Secret: The Forgotten Fighter Ace of the Korean War*
https://www.dvidshub.net/news/304237/top-secret-forgotten-fighter-ace-korean-war

Weiss, Wayne. Interview with Royce Williams (Transcript) 3/5/2016
http://video.flyingheritage.com/v/117085921/captain-e-royce-williams.htm

CHAPTER SEVENTEEN

CHARLES J. LORING
The Ultimate Sacrifice

By mid-1951 the Korean War had entered a period of relative stalemate, with back and forth engagements to gain territory. When Gen. Dwight D. Eisenhower resigned as the Supreme Commander of the North Atlantic Treaty Organization (NATO) in June 1952, Gen. Matthew Ridgway was transferred from Korea to Europe as Eisenhower's replacement and Gen. Mark Clark was given overall command of the UN forces as a replacement for Ridgway.

Although some, like General James Van Fleet, commander of the US Eighth Army, advocated for a renewed offensive into North Korean territory, Clark repeatedly overruled Van Fleet in order to minimize UN losses during the peace talks in Panmunjom.

In early September 1952, Van Fleet submitted tentative plans for Operation *Showdown*, a small-scale offensive to seize several ridges and push the Chinese Peoples Volunteer Army (PVA) defensive line back to improve the defensive line of the US 7th Infantry Division north of Kunhwa, South Korea.

As the negotiations at Panmunjom began to fall apart, primarily due to Sino-North Korean insistence that all prisoners of war be repatriated to their respective original countries regardless of whether they wished to be or not, they were met by strong opposition from the United States and South Korea.

On 8 October 1952, when truce negotiations officially ceased, Clark gave his consent to Operation *Showdown* the same day. The plan called for simultaneous attacks on both Triangle Hill and Sniper

Forgotten No More

Ridge. At 4 am on October 14, 1952, following two days of preliminary air strikes, the attack began.

Along the ridges, the Chinese had amassed 133 large-caliber guns, 24 BM-13 rocket launchers, and 47 anti-aircraft guns to defend their artillery. This massed firepower began decimating UN troops.

It was the largest Chinese artillery operation during the Korean War and the site was so heavily protected that, after 39 days of fighting, ground troops were unable to successfully capture the heavily guarded emplacement, so the decision was made to make an air attack.

On November 22, 1952, Major Charles Loring was tasked with leading a flight of three other F-80 *Shooting Star* fighter-bombers of the 80th Fighter-Bomber Squadron on a close support mission to bomb the position. Loring, a decorated combat pilot and WW II veteran was a good choice to lead the mission.

Born in Portland, Maine on October 2, 1918, Charles Joseph Loring Jr. was the oldest of 4 children born to Charles J. Loring Sr. and Mary Irene (Cronin) Loring, although one younger brother died as an infant. He and his brother Harold and sister Margaret Mary grew up in Portland and he attended Cheverus Catholic High School where he graduated in June 1937.

He hoped for a career as a professional boxer, but the outbreak of

WW II in September 1939, and America's entry on December 7, 1941 changed his plans and he enlisted in the US Army on March 16, 1942, at the age of 23.

In May, Loring was accepted as an aviation cadet in the Army Air Force and was assigned to Maxwell Field, Southeast Air Corps

Charles J. Loring

Training Center, at Montgomery, Alabama where he completed pre-flight training.

From there, Loring was sent to Douglas Field, California for Primary Flight Training, Greenville Mississippi for Basic Flight Training and Napier Field, Alabama for Advanced Flight Training, where he graduated on February 16, 1943, earning his Aviator's Wings and a reserve commission as a second lieutenant.

After taking leave, Loring was assigned to the 22nd Fighter Squadron, the "Red Hot Fighters" in late April, joining the squadron at Vega Baja Airfield in Puerto Rico. The squadron flew Bell P-39 *Airacobra* and Curtiss P-40 *Warhawk* fighters on anti-submarine and patrol missions guarding the Panama Canal.

When the navy took over anti-submarine duties, the squadron returned stateside to Morrison Field, Florida on May 27 1943.

Transferred to the 3rd Fighter Command in June 1943, the squadron began training for deployment to the European Theater of Operations (ETO) as a fighter-bomber squadron. The 22nd was assigned as part of the 36th Fighter Group in April 1944 and flew out of RAF Kingsnorth in Kent, England as part of the 9th Fighter Command, flying the Republic P-47 *Thunderbolt.*

In preparation for the Normandy invasion, the squadron flew missions that included strafing and dive-bombing armored vehicles, trains, bridges, buildings, factories, troop concentrations, gun emplacements, airfields, and other targets of opportunity.

The squadron also flew escort missions with Eighth Air Force Boeing B-17 *Flying Fortress* and Consolidated B-24 *Liberator* bombers. On D-Day, June 6, 1944, the squadron patrolled the air over the landing zones and flew close-support and interdiction missions.

On June 12, flying over Contances, France on a dive-bombing mission supporting the Allies breakout from Normandy, Loring, in actions his Distinguished Flying Cross citation would later describe as *"exceptional aerial skill and combat proficiency,"* flew through intense anti-aircraft and small arms fire to make repeated passes over a German convoy, *"destroying in all ten vehicles and causing heavy casualties in enemy personnel.*" One interesting note is that the official citation lists the award as posthumous.

In early August, Loring's aircraft was hit by ground fire, but luckily, despite his wounds, he was able to guide the crippled aircraft home. On his 55th mission, on Christmas Eve, December 24, 1944, Loring, now a first lieutenant, was flying a strafing mission over Belgium, in support of the Battle of the Bulge.

Making several passes through intense ground fire, his aircraft was again struck by enemy fire, but this time Loring was not as fortunate, and he crash landed behind enemy lines and was taken prisoner. Sent into the German interior, Loring would remain a P.O.W. until the camp was liberated on May 5, 1945.

He was returned stateside in June and after the war ended in September, his request to remain in the Army was granted, and in October he was promoted to captain.

Following the war, Loring held staff assignments at Victoria and Foster Fields, Texas as the Post Exchange (PX) officer and attended the Army Exchange School at Fort Oglethorpe, California. In 1946, he was sent to the Army Information School, at Carlisle

Charles J. Loring

Barracks, Pennsylvania to train in Public Affairs. Graduating with distinction, Loring was selected as an Instructor.

On September 18, 1947, the US Air Force became a separate Branch and Loring transferred over, serving at the newly formed Armed Forces Information School at Ft. Slocum, NY until 1951, with a temporary assignment in August 1949 to the Air Tactical School at Tyndall AFB, Florida.

When war erupted in Korea in June 1950, Loring volunteered for a combat assignment, but his request wasn't approved until February 1952 when he was assigned to the 8th Fighter-Bomber Wing, 5th Air Force, assigned to supervise pilot training.

Loring sailed for Korea on Decoration Day, May 25, 1952 and upon arriving, Loring was assigned to supervise training for replacement pilots before they were moved into combat units. During this time, he flew with both the 36th Fighter-Bomber Squadron and 80th Fighter-Bomber Squadron, while instructing newly arrived pilots.

Loring, newly promoted to major, requested assignment to fly combat missions and on July 3, he was appointed as Operations Officer for the 36th Fighter-Bomber Squadron, flying the Lockheed F-80 *Shooting Star*.

Armed with six 50 caliber machineguns and either eight 5" rockets or 2,000 pounds of bombs, the F-80 *Shooting Star* was the first USAF jet to see combat and with a range of 1,090 miles, a ceiling of 46,800 feet and speeds exceeding 500 mph, it was a formidable weapon.

Loring and his squadron flew close air support, air strikes and interdiction missions supporting UN ground troops in Korea. At some point, Loring transferred to the 80th Fighter-Bomber squadron.

By November 22, 1952, Loring had completed 50 combat missions, and the ground battle in Korea had developed into a stalemate, with the both sides firmly entrenched along the 38th Parallel. Throughout November, the UN forces had been fighting in Operation *Showdown* struggling to capture two targets: Triangle Hill and Sniper Ridge, both northwest of Kunwha, 20 miles north of the 38th Parallel.

That morning, Loring was leading a four-plane flight of F-80s on a ground support mission, Loring was briefed about the heavy guns and ground troops' situation. His flight diverted to dive-bomb the enemy gun positions. As he located the heavy guns, Loring took the lead on the bombing run lining up the artillery in his path.

However, the Chinese troops manning the anti-aircraft guns were exceptionally well-trained, and their firing was extremely accurate even at a distance and Loring's aircraft sustained significant damage to its fuselage which disabled the aircraft. The pilots of the other F-80 planes radioed to Loring to turn back and abort his mission.

Instead, Loring ceased radio contact and continued on his bombing run. Approaching the artillery batteries, he continued to take intense fire. Loring deliberately accelerated and then took a 45-degree angle directly towards the ground batteries as his wingmen looked on in horror.

What happened next is described in Loring's Medal of Honor citation;

"After verifying the location of the target, Maj. Loring rolled into his dive bomb run. Throughout the run, extremely accurate ground fire was directed on his aircraft. Disregarding the accuracy and intensity of the ground fire, Maj. Loring aggressively continued to press the attack until his aircraft was hit. At approximately 4,000 feet, he deliberately altered his course and aimed his diving aircraft at active gun emplacements concentrated on a ridge northwest of the briefed target, turned his aircraft 45 degrees to the left, pulled up in a deliberate, controlled maneuver, and elected to sacrifice his life by diving his aircraft directly into the midst of the enemy emplacements."

Loring crashed into the enemy position exploding on impact and completely destroying it. Loring was killed instantly, and his wingmen could not believe what they had witnessed. Their reports would lead to his being nominated and posthumously awarded the nation's highest military honor. His action that day saved countless numbers of UN troops.

Charles J. Loring

Loring became one of only four USAF airmen to be awarded the Medal of Honor during the Korean conflict when on May 5, 1954, President Dwight Eisenhower awarded him a posthumous Medal of Honor. The award was kept secret by the Air Force "to protect him from enemy reprisal" in the event that Major Loring had not died in the crash of his fighter but had been captured by the Chinese.

The Medal was presented to Mrs. Elsie Loring and her two daughters, Aldor and Charlene, by Secretary of the Air Force Harold E. Talbott, during a ceremony held at Bolling Air Force Base, Washington, D.C. on April 17, 1954. Limestone Army Airfield in Maine was renamed Loring Air Force Base, October 1, 1954.

Loring is memorialized by cenotaphs at both Arlington National Cemetery, Arlington, Virginia (Section MK – Grave 89) and Calvary Cemetery, South Portland, Maine. Loring's remains were never recovered after the crash and he is listed as "Missing in action, presumed dead."

Some speculate as to why Loring didn't bail out of his crippled aircraft. According to his father, Charles J. Loring, Sr., *"Charley was a stubborn man. He said he would never be a prisoner again. He was the kind of man who kept his word about everything."*

SOURCES:

Bamford, SMSgt. Hal. *Destined to Die* Airman Magazine- Journal of the US Air Force

Forgotten No More

Charles Joseph Loring, Jr. – Arlington National Cemetery website
http://www.arlingtoncemetery.net/cjloringjr.htm

Cloer, Lee. *A Hero's Last Mission in His P-80 Shooting Star*
https://duotechservices.com/a-heros-last-mission-in-his-p-80-
shooting-star

Medal of Honor, Major Charles Joseph Loring, Jr., United States Air Force
- https://www.thisdayinaviation.com/tag/charles-joseph-loring-jr/

CHAPTER EIGHTEEN

ARNE STENSLIE
Oldest Recipient of the Silver Star Medal

The Silver Star Medal is the United States Armed Forces' third-highest personal decoration for valor in combat. The Silver Star is the successor award to the "Citation Star" which was established by an Act of Congress on July 9, 1918, during World War I. On July 19, 1932, the Secretary of War approved the conversion of the "Citation Star" to the Silver Star Medal with the original "Citation Star" incorporated into the center of the medal's design.

Authorization for the Silver Star Medal was placed into law by an Act of Congress for the U.S. Navy on August 7, 1942, and an Act of Congress for the U.S. Army on December 15, 1942. The Silver Star Medal is awarded for gallantry, so long as the action does not justify the award of one of the next higher valor awards: The Distinguished Service Cross, the Navy Cross, the Air Force Cross, or the Coast Guard Cross.

The gallantry displayed must have taken place while in action against an enemy of the United States, while engaged in military operations involving conflict with an opposing foreign force, or while serving with friendly foreign forces engaged in an armed conflict against an opposing armed force in which the United States is not a belligerent party.

On November 26, 1950, near Kuchangdong, South Korea, Master Sergeant Arne Stenslie ventured out alone under intense mortar and small arms fire in an effort to identify soldiers flanking his position. His efforts would result in the award of the Silver Star, making him at age 60, the oldest individual to earn the medal.

Forgotten No More

Arne Stenslie was born in Gjovik, Norway on December 10, 1890 and emigrated to the United States with his family. He was living in Devils Lake, North Dakota when the United States entered WW I with a declaration of war on April 6, 1917. Stenslie enlisted as a private in Company D, 2nd North Dakota Infantry of the state's National Guard on June 30, 1917.

In response to President Woodrow Wilson's order for a partial mobilization in late March, in response to Germany resuming unrestricted submarine warfare, North Dakota called up its National Guard on March 26, 1917. The 2nd Regiment had only been home from service on the Mexican border for 40 days.

3,700 North Dakota men, guardsmen and volunteers were called up with 2,051 assigned to the 1st Regiment and the remaining 1,649 men assigned to the 2nd Regiment. On September 19, both regiments were sent to Camp Greene, North Carolina assigned to the 34th Infantry Division.

In October 1917, the 2nd Regiment was disbanded, and its five infantry companies were absorbed into the 1st Regiment and re-designated as the 164th Infantry.

The need to get troops to France quickly reduced the time for training with Stenslie and others only receiving nine days of marksmanship training with their rifles. On November 16, the 164th embarked from Long Island, NY for France. After a brief stop in England, the 164th arrived at the 41st Infantry Division's camp at La Courtine, France.

The 41st Division would end up providing replacements for other divisions. Most of the privates in the 164th Regiment were immediately

transferred to the First Division. Stenslie was transferred to the 164th Headquarters Company.

The 164th Regiment lost 278 men in the war. One hundred seventy-six died in battle, 62 died of wounds, and the remainder succumbed to disease. Nearly 650 men suffered battle wounds.

Arne Stenslie

The 41st Division returned Camp Dix, New Jersey on February 28, 1919 and Stenslie was honorably discharged on March 11, 1919 and returned home to Devils Lake.

After trying farming for several years, Stenslie opted for a military career and was commissioned in the Officers Reserve Corps (ORC) in 1924. To further his military education, he attended the annual North Dakota National Guard field training exercises held at Camp Grafton without pay.

On May 27, 1933, Stenslie, now a captain, was put in command of Company 764, Civilian Conservation Corps (CCC), a public works relief effort that operated in the U.S. from 1933 to 1942.

As part of the New Deal, unemployed and unmarried men between the ages of 18 to 25 were recruited into the CCC and provided manual labor jobs to develop the natural resources in rural lands owned by federal, state, and local governments as part of President Franklin Roosevelt's effort to provide relief for American families struggling to find work and make ends meet during the Great Depression.

On October 16, Company 764 relocated to Camp Lost Corner in Pope County, Arkansas where they were put to work building fire roads, planting trees, soil conservation projects and fighting fires.

Stenslie remained with the CCC until the outbreak of WW II, when he was appointed Provost Marshal of St. Louis, Missouri. Deemed too old for service overseas, he remained stateside for the duration of WW II. From 1946 -1949, Stenslie served with the Occupation forces in Korea.

Stenslie returned stateside and was stationed at Camp Stoneman, outside Pittsburg, California, when war broke out in Korea on June 25, 1950. Stenslie wanted to get in the fight, but he had reached the mandatory retirement age of 60.

On June 30, 1950, Stenslie retired from the U.S. Army with the rank of major. The following day, July 1, Stenslie enlisted as a private with the assurance that he'd be assigned to the 2nd Infantry

Forgotten No More

Division at Fort Lewis, Washington. The unit was currently preparing for deployment to Korea.

The 2nd Infantry Division, was assigned to the Far East Command as part of the US Eighth Army. The division arrived in Korea, via Pusan on July 23, becoming the first unit to reach Korea directly from the United States. Since the 2nd Infantry Division was at full strength, its three infantry regiments were quickly moved into the defensive lines of the Pusan Perimeter. On August 24, they replaced the 24th Infantry Division which was woefully understrength (down to 45% strength).

But, their new defensive sector was plagued by refugees heading south. Enemy infiltrations behind friendly lines disrupted command posts as well as resupply routes, and the 2nd Infantry's sector covered some 35 miles, stretching from the juncture of the Naktong and Nam Rivers in the south to the town of Hyonpung in the north. Opposing them were the 105th Armored as well as the 4th and 8th Infantry Divisions of the North Korea People's Army (NKPA).

Stenslie, promoted to Master Sergeant was assigned to 23rd Infantry Regiment. For his leadership and service with the division, Stenslie became known as "Mr. Second Division".

He earned his greatest distinction in the firefight that began on the night of November 26, 1950 near Pyongyang, North Korea, that followed Chinese intervention.

Stenslie assembled a makeshift company of cooks,

truck drivers, clerks, who in two ferocious nights of fighting saved the 23rd Infantry's command post from being overrun by the unceasing charges by the Communist Chinese troops.

For his actions, Stenslie was awarded the Silver Star Medal. As the medal's citation stated *"Master Sergeant Stenslie organized and led the defense of a frontline position near Kuchangdon. With complete disregard for his safety, Sergeant Stenslie personally verified the positions of enemy troops and led an attack. Later he heard American voices several hundred yards to the flank of his position. Again, the sergeant went out by himself during heavy enemy mortar and small arms fire in an effort to lead the cut-off men to friendly positions."*

As Stenslie would recall later in an October 1954 newspaper interview; *"One bunch, you could see their rifles, came at us through a dim valley. You could not tell who was who. We didn't even know our own men. I couldn't order a man to go out there and find out who they were. That wouldn't have been right. I was the oldest man, and I discovered them to be Chinese preparing to attack."*

During the fight he was seriously wounded when he was shot in the face and he spent his 60th birthday in the hospital in Osaki, Japan, recovering from wounds.

After returning from the hospital, he was assigned to the job of giving orientation talks to replacements, and he says that in the next two years he talked to more than 35,000 men, many of them were Koreans whom he addressed in their native tongue.

He vowed that he would not leave Korea until an armistice was signed or that the Second Division was sent home. He was able to keep both promises.

The Armistice Agreement was signed by representatives of the United States, United Nations, North Korea and Communist China on July 27, 1953 in P'anmunjom.

At the final review of the 2nd Division at Inchon, Korea, Stenslie was presented the Legion of Merit by General Maxwell Taylor, then the commander of the U. S. 8th Army.

Forgotten No More

When he returned with the division to Fort Lewis, Washington in late September 1953, Stenslie became the only individual to serve with the 2nd Division for its entire deployment to Korea. The division paid a high price, with 7,094 killed. Its awards included the Presidential Unit Citation, the highest award given to units.

Stenslie retired from the Army a second time, at the age of 66, on May 17, 1957 as a reserve lieutenant colonel with 33 years of service, including 27 consecutive months in Korea.

As a final salute, Gen. Taylor, personally presented him with his retired orders, and also presented the 5'5 officer with the second Oak Leaf Cluster to add to his Army Commendation Medal

He was awarded the following decorations: Silver Star Medal, Legion of Merit, Army Commendation Medal, with two Oak Leaf clusters, Purple Heart, Good Conduct Medal, the Distinguished Unit Citation and one Oak Leaf Cluster, the Meritorious Unit Commendation, and his Korean· Service Medal with 10 Bronze Stars.

Stenslie died unexpectedly at his Santa Ana, California home on February 29, 1968 and was buried with full military honors at Fairhaven Memorial Park.

Lt. Col. Stenslie is the only man who is authorized ten stars on the Korean Service Ribbon, including stars for the Battle of Pusan Perimeter, Battle of the Ch'ongch'on River, First and Second Battles of Wonju, Battle of Chipyong-ni, Battle of Bloody Ridge and the Battle of Heartbreak Ridge.

SOURCES:

164th Infantry News – March 1968
https://commons.und.edu/cgi/viewcontent.cgi?article=1089&
context=infantry-documents

Johnson, Ed. *Old Sarge is Humble Man after 32 Years Army Service -
The Key West Citizen (FL) Oct. 9, 1954*

Arne Stenslie

Mr. Second Division Is Home from Korean Front He's 63 and Has Served with Distinction in Army for 32 Years – Dixon Evening Telegraph (IL) Oct. 9, 1954

CHAPTER NINETEEN

STAFF SERGEANT RECKLESS
Dickin Medal Awardee, 2 Purple Hearts

On August 31, 1959, the 5th Marine Regiment gathered on the parade ground at Camp Pendleton, California to honor the promotion of one of their own to the rank of staff-sergeant.

It was a crisp, clear California morning as flags snapped in the ocean breeze and the Marine band played Semper Fidelis and the Marine Corps Hymn. The regiment passed in review for over 3,000 guests. Then Gen. Randolph McCall Pate, the Commandant of the Marine Corps, stepped forward to promote the Marine, a combat veteran of Korea.

The Marine being promoted was out of the ordinary in several respects. First, she was a female. Second, she was just turned 11 years old. Finally, she stood at attention on all four legs. Sgt. Reckless was a horse.

Forgotten No More

Sgt. Reckless, the Heroine of the Battle for Outpost Vegas, stood proudly as Gen. Pate pinned the chevrons on her blanket, next to her two Purple Hearts and Good Conduct Medal.

Sgt. Reckless began life as "Flame in the Morning" a chestnut Mongolian pony born to the racehorse "Flame" in June 1948. She was left an orphan when he mother died the following week and would most likely have followed in her mother's hoofprints had the Korean War not intruded.

Destroyed in the war, the Sinseul-Dong Racetrack in Seoul was transformed into a US Army airfield, but some owners still kept horses there, hoping for a resumption of racing. Reckless was three years old when 2Lt. Eric Theodore "Pete" Pedersen arrived in a jeep with two other Marines, Sgt. Willard Berry and Cpl. Philip Carter, in October 1952.

Pedersen, a 32-year-old rancher from California, had enlisted in the Corps as a private on December 8, 1938 and had served during WW II, earning a battlefield commission. Now he commanded the Recoilless Rifle Platoon of the 5th Marine's Anti-tank Company.

The terrain that the 5th Marines was currently operating was a trio of outposts atop steep mountains nicknamed Reno, Vegas and Carson. The outposts were inaccessible to motorized vehicles.

Pedersen had persuaded the regimental commander, Col. Eustace Smock, to let him experiment with using a horse as an ammunition carrier. Ammunition for the M-20 75-mm. Recoilless Rifle weighed 20-22 lbs. per shell and Marines could only carry 2-3 shells up the steep incline. It was hoped that a horse might carry up to ten shells.

Pedersen met with Kim Huk Moon, who though reluctant to sell the horse, needed money for a prosthetic leg for his sister who had lost her left leg in a landmine explosion. Using $250 of his own money, Pedersen purchased the horse on October 26, 1952.

Enlisted as a Private First Class, Serial # H-1, and renamed "Reckless", slang for the recoilless rifle, she was trained by Gunnery Sgt. Joseph Latham, an Alabama farmer, who taught her how to navigate barbed wire, how to recognize commo wire, and how to "hit the deck" and kneel when under fire. She learned to run for the bunker when the shout of "incoming" was heard and she was quick to learn new routes and only needed to be shown a few times before being able to make the trip unaccompanied.

Private First Class Monroe Coleman, also experienced with horses, was selected as her primary caretaker and companion, and the unit's corpsman, Navy Hospitalman First Class George "Doc" Mitchell provided medical care.

Reckless had her baptism of fire at a place called "Hedley's crotch", between the villages of Changdan and Kwakchen, in November 1952. Carrying six shells uphill under fire, she was initially skittish, but rapidly became accustomed to gunfire and the noise of the 75mm, which had an ear-jarring blast.

With winter vegetation scarce, Reckless soon also became accustomed to a Marine diet, supplemented by Wheaties, Graham crackers, scrambled eggs, Coca-Cola and the occasional beer. She had the run of the camp and was promoted to corporal in January 1953.

By March 1953, the 5th Marines, part of the 1st Marine Division, I Corps, were assigned a 35-mile (56 km) sector to defend on the Main Line of Resistance (MLR). The 1st Battalion, 5th Marines was tasked with defending the "Nevada Cities", reportedly named by Lieutenant Colonel Tony Caputa because "it's a gamble if we can hold them."

The Battle for Outpost Vegas, one of the last major offensives of the war, began on the night of March 26 with a Chinese PVA (Peoples Volunteer Army) attack against outposts Vegas, Carson, and Reno. The Chinese hoped to capture the Nevada Cities north of the MLR in order to gain leverage at the Panmunjom peace talks. If the PVA gained a victory there, it would put pressure on the UN negotiators at the talks.

That first night of the battle Reckless was credited with making 51 round trips up the hill, carrying 386 recoilless rounds (9,000 pounds), traveling 35 miles and working from dusk to dawn. Familiar with the route, Reckless, unaccompanied, carried ammunition up the hill and wounded down.

Forgotten No More

After eight hours of fighting in and around the Nevada Cities, the PVA had endured an estimated 600 casualties, 4 times more than that of the Marines loss of 150.

Over the next three days, Reckless worked tirelessly, under fire, the Marines covering her with their flak jackets to create an "armored horse" to provide cover as they ascended the hills. Despite being twice wounded by shrapnel, Reckless continued carrying ammo, both recoilless and mortar rounds to the beleaguered Marines.

Reckless remained on the line with her Marines for 68 days, frequently coming under fire. When not at the front, she performed other tasks like laying down communication wire from reels attached to her pack, stringing as much as twelve men.

In early May, the 1st Marine Division was replaced by the Turkish Brigade, and the Marines went into reserve after almost a week of renewed heavy fighting in and around the "Nevada Cities" outposts.

Cpl. Reckless became the first horse in Marine Corps history to make an amphibious landing. The 5th Marines were assigned to participate in a 10-day amphibious exercise commencing on May 8, 1953, moving from Camp Casey near Dongducheon, 40 miles north of Seoul to Inchon. Despite getting seasick aboard the USS *Talladega* (APA-208) and being delayed by a storm, she landed at Inchon aboard LST #1084 (Landing Ship – Tank).

On July 27, 1953, an armistice was signed ending hostilities, signed by U.S. Army Lieutenant General William Harrison, Jr. representing the United Nations Command (UNC), and North Korean General Nam Il representing the Korean People's Army (KPA), and the Chinese People's Volunteer Army (PVA). South Korea did not sign.

The armistice called for the creation of a Demilitarized Zone (DMZ) between North and South Korea, to be 4,000 yards wide along a 155-mile front, and for it to be patrolled by "civil police".

Camp Semper Fidelis was built to house the First Provisional DMZ Police Company, formed on September 4, 1953, with each regiment of the First Marine Division providing 25 enlisted men and an officer. On September 21, the Police Company was attached to the 5th Marines.

Reckless remained on active duty with the Marines, and on April 10, 1954, Major General Randolph Pate, Commanding General of the 1st Marine Division, and the highest ranked Marine in Korea, promoted Reckless to sergeant in a formal ceremony, and she was presented with a red and gold blanket displaying her rank and awards.

Afraid that she might be left behind, an article in the Saturday Evening Post on April 17, 1954 resulted in a campaign to bring her home to the United States. The article was written by Lt. Col. Andrew Geer, Commanding Officer of the 2nd Battalion, 5th Marines, and an accomplished screenwriter.

Stan Coppel, an executive at Pacific Transport Lines read the article and offered Reckless free passage aboard one of his company's ships. Prior to her departure from Korea, a farewell ceremony, complete with marching band, was held during the half-time of an Army-Marine football game.

A 1st Marine Aircraft Wing transport airlifted Reckless from Korea to Yokohama, Japan on October 16, 1954, where she departed for San Francisco on October 22, aboard the *SS Pacific Transport*. Although scheduled to dock in San Francisco, a typhoon delayed arrival until November 9.

Reckless was greeted as a hero on arrival with hundreds on the pier, including California Governor Goodwin Knight. Although the US Customs Bureau presented no difficulties, the US Dept. of Agriculture was another matter, demanding a medical check and blood test be completed before she would be allowed to disembark.

November 10 is the birthday of the Marine Corps and Reckless was scheduled to be the guest of honor at the Marine Corps' 179th Birthday Ball that evening. High level phone calls between the Marines and Agriculture officials in Washington DC reached an agreement to take the tests, but allow her off the ship before the results were in.

Led down the gangplank by Lt. Pendersen, Reckless attended the birthday bash, riding in an elevator for the first time, and dining

Forgotten No More

on cake and several flower arrangements. She also made several personal appearances, including on television.

Reckless moved with the 5th Marines to Camp Pendleton, outside San Diego, California, where she continued to serve, representing the Marine Corps at change of command ceremonies, promotions and retirements, official functions and civilian parades.

A second *Saturday Evening Post* article on October 22, 1955, and a book, *Reckless: Pride of the Marines* published in 1955, both written by Lt. Col. Geer, solidified her fame, outshining other animal heroes like Lassie and Rin Tin Tin.

On August 31, 1959, Reckless was promoted to the rank of Staff Sergeant in a ceremony presided over by Gen. Pate, now the 21st Commandant of the Marine Corps, and was honored with a 19-gun salute and a 1,700-man parade comprised of men from her wartime unit.

As Pate recalled his first sight of Reckless, he stated *"I was surprised at her beauty and intelligence, and believe it or not, her esprit de corps. Like any other Marine, she was enjoying a bottle of beer with her comrades...It was obvious the Marines loved her."*

During her time in the Marines, Reckless delivered three colts, Fearless in 1957, Dauntless in 1959 and Chesty in 1964. A filly that died shortly after birth remained unnamed.

Staff Sergeant Reckless retired from active duty with full military honors, on November 10, 1960, the Corps 185th birthday. In lieu of retirement pay, Reckless was provided free quarters and rations for life.

Plagued by arthritis, Chestnut fell into a barbed wire fence, and she died under sedation while her wounds were being treated on May 13, 1968. She was buried at the Camp Pendleton stables with full military honors.

In 1997, Life Magazine ran a special edition celebrating America's Top 100 Heroes, and listed along with Jefferson, Lincoln, Washington, Eleanor Roosevelt, Martin Luthor King Jr. and Mother Teresa was Sgt. Reckless.

Staff Sergeant Reckless

Reckless was honored with a 10-foot bronze statue of her by sculptor Jocelyn Russell, at the National Museum of the Marine Corps in Quantico, Virginia, on July 26, 2013. A similar statue by the same sculptor was dedicated at Camp Pendleton on October 26, 2016.

On July 27, 2016, the 63rd anniversary of the end of the Korean War, Sgt. Reckless was posthumously awarded the Dickin Medal, the animal equivalent to Britain's Victoria Cross. US Embassy attaché Lt. Col. Michael Skaggs accepted the award. In November 2019, she became one of the first recipients of the new American equivalent of the Dickin Medal, the Animals in War & Peace Medal of Bravery.

But perhaps her greatest tribute is the simplest. Engraved on a plaque at the entrance to Stepp Stables at Camp Pendleton; *"She Wasn't a Horse, she was a Marine."*

SOURCES:

Forgotten No More

Futini, John Stephen. *The Forgotten War: A four-legged corporal serves the Marines* Napa Valley Register (Ca). Jan. 28, 2018
https://napavalleyregister.com/community/calistogan/news/opinion/mailbag/the-forgotten-war-a-four-legged-corporal-serves-the-marines/article_f84b70ed-8deb-5b0a-8c33-35fb44373407.html

Horse Stars Hall of Fame
http://www.horsestarhalloffame.org/inductees/64/staff_sergeant_reckless.aspx

Hutton, Robin Sgt. Reckless: America's War Horse Simon and Schuster (NY) 2014

Ritchie, Erika I. Staff Sgt. Reckless wasn't just a horse, she was a Marine who served in Korean War Orange County Register (Ca) Sept. 2, 2016

Made in the USA
Columbia, SC
14 December 2021

51491214R00114